1987

BRANDING: A KEY MARKETING TOOL

BRANDING:
A KEY MARKETING TOOL

Edited by

John M. Murphy
Chairman, Interbrand/Novamark Group, London
Offices in New York

McGraw-Hill Book Company

New York   St. Louis   San Francisco

First published 1987

Published by
THE MACMILLAN PRESS LTD
Houndmills, Basingstoke, Hampshire RG21 2XS
and London
Companies and representatives
throughout the world

Published in the United States and its
dependencies by McGraw-Hill Book Company,
New York, N.Y., by arrangement with The
Macmillan Press Ltd.

Filmsetting by Vantage Photosetting Co. Ltd
Eastleigh and Southampton

Printed in Hong Kong

Library of Congress Cataloging-in-Publication Data

Branding : a key marketing tool.

Includes index.
1. Brand name products.   2. Business names.
3. Marketing.   I. Murphy, John M., 1944–   .
HD69.B7B73   1987   658.8'27   86–27797

ISBN 0-07-044055-7

Contents

List of Plates

Notes on the Contributors

Tom Blackett is a Director of Novamark International and has extensive experience in marketing consultancy, new product development and marketing research.

Vincent Carratu was formerly with The Company Fraud Department at New Scotland Yard but now runs The Carratu Group, a leading investigation agency.

Leslie Collins is a psychologist and now has his own marketing research and consultancy practice in London, ICR Ltd.

Graham Denton is founder and President of The Initiatives Group, one of the largest new product development consultancies in North America.

John Diefenbach is Chief Executive Officer of Landor Associates of San Francisco, one of the leading US design firms.

Clarke Graham is a trademark lawyer. He was born in Australia and is the Senior Partner in Markforce Associates, a British trademark legal practice.

Dr Robert Grayson is a marketing and management consultant and is Adjunct Professor of Marketing at the New York University Graduate School of Business Administration.

Laurence Hefter teaches trademark law at George Washington University Law School and is a Senior Partner in the firm of Finnegan, Henderson, Farabow, Garrett & Dunner.

Mervyn Kurlansky is a senior partner of Pentagram, one of Britain's leading design consultancies.

Terry Leahy is Marketing Director of Tesco, one of Britain's leading and most successful retail groups.

Dr Klaus Morwind is a member of the managing board of Henkel KGaA of

Dusseldorf and is particularly responsible for Henkel's worldwide export business in detergents.

John M. Murphy (editor) is the founder of Novamark International, London and Chairman of the worldwide Interbrand/Novamark Group of companies, leading specialists in the development of brand names.

Terry Nolan has over thirty years' experience in the motor industry. He is currently responsible for both short- and long-term planning at Austin Rover.

Terry Oliver was born in England but has lived in Tokyo for many years. He is Joint Managing Director of Interbrand Japan.

Mark Peroff is a US attorney and is a partner in Bierman, Peroff & Muserlian, a New York firm of trademark lawyers.

Adrian Room is Vice-President of The Names Society and a prolific author on the history of brand names.

Barbara Sudovar is Executive Director of Almed Focus, a division of Almed Inc. She was formerly Manager of New Product Development for Pfizer-Roerig in New York.

Russell Taylor is Managing Director of Dyno-Rod plc, a company which pioneered specialist plumbing services in the UK.

Steve Winram is a member of Saatchi & Saatchi's corporate finance team and has been particularly involved with the company's strategic development.

Preface

Coca-Cola's most valuable assets are its brands. The same is true for scores of major corporations around the world. Brands are the invisible assets of corporations. They seldom appear in balance sheets and are frequently guarded less jealously than are property assets, for example. Even when brands are sold, often for enormous sums, the proceeds are hidden under some mystifying heading such as 'goodwill'. When a company is acquired value is attached to real estate (which is frequently sold off), to management teams (who are frequently sacked), and to plant (which effectively may have no real value whatsoever) yet the brands themselves, the core of the business and the reason it is being acquired, are unacknowledged.

In the world of marketing we have generally failed to recognise fully the value of brands. We have failed too to recognise that names are at the heart of a brand's personality. They are the one aspect of a brand which never changes, they are the most readily protected component of a brand and they are the single most potent means of differentiating one product from another.

The paradox of the brand name is unconsciously acknowledged by those company chairmen who develop their own brand names. They will leave concept development and market research to their marketing teams, product and packaging design to the designers, origination of advertising and the selection of media to the advertising agency but the name itself, the core of the product's identity and personality and the one component of the product mix which will never be altered, is developed by the Chairman single-handedly and in the shower. Or by the Chairman's wife, niece, downstairs maid or shoe-shine boy. Somehow it seems that launching a new product involves paternity. It is also somewhat mystical. A high priest is required for the laying on of hands and who better to do this than the Chairman?

Brands, therefore, are important and valuable assets which are frequently underacknowledged and misunderstood. The processes of new brand development and of brand management are similarly mysterious. This is not to say that certain important components of the branding process – for example design, market research, advertising – are inadequately developed or unprofessional. Rather, that integrating these particular areas of expertise into a systematic and coherent approach to branding frequently relies mainly on intuition. Furthermore, certain key parts of the branding process – for instance brand name development – have generally in the past been tackled haphazardly and, at times, illogically.

Of course, in the complex worlds of packaged goods and consumer products, of automobiles and financial services, we have many tools other than the brand name with which to distinguish our products and invest them with personality. Foremost amongst these are advertising, promotion and packaging. Other ways in which we can differentiate our product from that of the competition include such things as product formulation, delivery systems, sizes, colour, smell, shape, etc. However, once we have put all these elements to work and blended them together into a brand, it is sensible to give the brand a name which is as strong, appropriate and protectable as possible, for it is within this identity that the core attributes of the product or service ultimately reside.

It is this combining of multiple messages within the framework of a brand name that is central to the development of brand personality. And make no mistake about it, it is something that is difficult and becomes more difficult as time goes by, as markets become more cluttered, as competitive pressures increase, as international marketing becomes more necessary, and as the sheer volume of registered trademarks grows around the world.

Yet the power of a good brand is simply staggering. Consider for a moment the awesome reach, the ability to communicate, the sheer financial value of some of the world's great brand names. From Brazil to Canada, from Japan to the United Kingdom brand names speak out loud and clear; they conjure up images, they work at both conscious and subconscious levels, they cut across the barriers of race, religion, colour and language – they are truly the universal communicators.

The objective of this book is to bring branding into perspective in terms of its value, importance and its rôle in marketing. It also covers in some detail such areas as licensing, counterfeiting, line extension, the protection and care of brand names, and the creation of new brands and trademarks – areas of critical importance today to all of us involved in the key areas of new product development, brand management, marketing and advertising.

This book will also provide you with valuable insights based upon the real-life experience of brand owners, brand managers, retailers, advertising agents, packaging designers and consultants from around the world.

We hope you will find *Branding* both stimulating and informative.

London JOHN M. MURPHY

NOTES

1. Certain names used in this book may be registered trademarks in some countries but generic names in others. The use of a name in one form or the other implies no judgement as to its legal status in any particular country.
2. In the United Kingdom 'trade mark' is normally written as two words but in the USA as a single word. In general we have, for the sake of consistency, adopted the American convention – 'trademark' – in this book.

1 What Is Branding?

JOHN M. MURPHY

INTRODUCTION

Since the earliest times producers of goods have used their brands or marks to distinguish their products. Pride in their products has no doubt played a part in this. More particularly, by identifying their products they have provided purchasers with a means of recognising and specifying them should they wish to repurchase or recommend the products to others.

The use of brands by producers has developed considerably over the centuries and especially in the last century. But the function of a brand as distinguishing the goods of one producer from those of another and of thus allowing consumers freedom of choice has remained unaltered.

The ways in which brands have developed over the years are essentially threefold. First, legal systems have recognised the value of brands to both producers and consumers. Most countries in the world now recognise that intellectual property – trademarks, patents, designs, copyright – is property in a very real sense and therefore confer rights on the owners of such property. Secondly, the concept of branded goods has been extended successfully to embrace services. Thus the providers of financial, retail or other services can now generally treat them as branded products, provided they are distinguished from those of competitors. Thus service brands now generally enjoy the same statutory rights as product brands. Thirdly, and perhaps most importantly, the ways in which branded products or services are distinguished from one another have increasingly come to embrace non-tangible factors, as well as such real factors as size, shape, make-up and price. The brand qualities which consumers rely upon in making a choice between brands have become increasingly subtle and, at times, fickle. Cigarette *A* may be virtually indistinguishable from Cigarette *B* yet outsell it ten to one; a fragrance costing $5 a bottle may be outsold by another fragrance with very similar physical characteristics but which sells at $50 a bottle.

Thus modern, sophisticated branding is now concerned increasingly with a brand's '*gestalt*', with assembling together and maintaining a mix of values, both tangible and intangible, which are relevant to consumers and which

1

meaningfully and appropriately distinguish one supplier's brand from that of another.

Intangible factors are, however, very difficult to estimate even individually. When a number of such elements are blended together to form that unique creation, a branded product, evaluation of these separate but interrelated constituents is far from easy. Prior to a brand's launch, measuring its likely success is notoriously difficult. Even after launch it may not be possible to ascertain with any certainty the reasons for the success or failure of a brand.

In practical terms this has led companies to use a number of alternative strategies for developing new brands. The most obvious one is that of developing 'me too' products. Every successful new brand attracts a flock of imitators similar in concept, get-up, brand name and function to the original. Such 'me too' brands frequently have little chance of competing seriously with the original brand unless, for example, they are able to offer a substantial price advantage. They do, however, offer a producer a low-risk opportunity to enter a market at low cost and secure a modest market share.

Another common approach is that of pseudo-sophistication. Every possible attribute of a new brand is measured whether it is relevant or not and whether such measurement provides data of any value in making decisions. Moreover, as such research is frequently done among consumers whose experience is limited to the existing brands on the market and who tend, therefore, to react most favourably in a research situation to the familiar and, frequently, the banal, this approach tends, unless it is handled very skilfully, to lead to unexciting and uninspired brands. Such research does, however, provide good excuses in the event of failure!

Other organisations, especially those in areas such as fashion and fragrances, frequently view branding entirely as a creative or artistic process largely unfettered by research considerations.

Perhaps the most appropriate and successful approach to the development of new brands is the pragmatic one – try to identify new brands with some measure of distinctiveness and consumer appeal and which are not simply 'me too' products, use appropriate research techniques to measure the brand's likely market success, recognise that branding does have a strong creative element and encourage creativity and flair. But recognise too that successful new brands, due to their very intangibility, can never be guaranteed to be successes. The chances of success can be significantly increased though.

In a sense, branding consists of imposing one's will on the consumer. Consumers would never have conceived of a fragrance called Charlie – indeed the culture of branding when Charlie was first launched was one where most new fragrances carried feminine, elegant, French names and consumers at that time would have specified that any new brand must meet these parameters. Yet Charlie struck a chord with consumers around the world which was attractive and unique. The brand embodied a set of values and attributes which were appropriate, which stimulated consumer interest, which distinguished the brand from others and created a unique piece of property for its owners. Charlie, then, might be seen as a 'power brand', a uniquely successful blending together of qualities and attributes both tangible and intangible. The brand offers a unique set of values and attributes which are appealing and which people are prepared to purchase. Furthermore, there is no doubt that Charlie represents for Revlon a valuable asset which has enduring and international appeal.

POWER BRANDS

Power brands are those brands which are particularly well adapted to the environment and which thus survive and flourish. They are the ultimate examples of an organisation's marketing skills – their finest and most valuable productions. Power brands can apply to either goods or services, can act as corporate names as well as product brand names and can apply to very specific products or to ranges of related products. What they have in common is that they all embrace products which are well priced and offer good and consistent quality to consumers. Hence the brand, in a sense, acts as a credible guarantee for that product or service allowing the consumer clearly to identify and specify products which genuinely offer 'added value'.

The term 'marketing mix' is frequently used to describe the process of developing a new brand and it is apt. Essentially a provider of a product or service assembles a series of attributes and blends these together in a unique way. It is a little like cooking – part of the skill is in the selection of the elements in the mix, part in the blending and cooking and part in the presentation. A good cook produces good and consistent results which are constantly in demand.

The ingredients in a brand constitute the product itself, the packaging, the brand name, the promotion, the advertising and the overall presentation. The brand is therefore a synthesis of all these elements, physical, aesthetic, rational and emotional. Essentially, the end result must be not only appropriate but differentiated from the brands of competitors – the consumer has to have a reason to choose one brand over all others.

Branding consists, then, of the development and maintenance of sets of product attributes and values which are coherent, appropriate, distinctive, protectable and appealing to consumers. Marketing is a broader function which includes branding and concerns the development and implementation of strategies for moving products or services from the producer to the consumer in a profitable fashion. Advertising is a narrower function within marketing which is concerned with the use of media to inform and stimulate consumers that products or services, branded or otherwise, are available for them to purchase.

IMPORTANCE OF BRANDS

Companies who invent new brands are able generally to defend them from blatant copying in a variety of ways, though not normally from broad imitation. If a brand is a good one consumers will purchase it and it becomes a valuable asset. But its asset value derives from more than just its ability to attract sales. The very fact that consumers perceive a brand as embracing a set of values which they can specify means that they will reject, or tend to reject, alternatives which are presented to them that perhaps may not possess all these values. Brands are therefore enduring assets as long as they are kept in good shape and continue to offer consumers the values they require.

In practice producers of goods or services generally do not interact directly with their consumers. Kodak films are normally sold through chemists or kiosks or mail order; Formica laminates are sold by hardware stores or as components in fitted kitchens; Pan-Am airline tickets are retailed through travel agents. Thus the producer, the brand owner, constantly faces the possibility that, at point of sale, his efforts to develop branded products which attract strong consumer interest will come to nothing. If Heinz Baked Beans are unavailable or a penny or two more expensive than Safeway's own-brand baked beans, the own-brand product may well suffice; if Pan-Am Clipper Class is fully booked the traveller will readily settle for British Airways Club; if Ford's Sierra is on six weeks delivery and the equivalent Audi is available from stock then the Audi may do just as well. Few brands are so powerful as to protect the brand owner against the persuasiveness of a substantially lower price or a much better delivery. For this reason the marketing function is normally concerned with ensuring that a company's brands are not handicapped by such factors.

But what the successful brand does is tip the balance slightly in favour of the producer or at least ensure that the balance does not rest entirely with the retailer. H. G. Wells described this process as 'reaching over the shoulder of the retailer straight to the consumer'. The brand allows the brand owner to prevent his product simply becoming a commodity which is bought by an intermediary, mainly a major retailing or distribution chain, simply on the basis of the market forces operating at a particular time.

But brands do more than just protect the producer from the depredations of the retailer – in a very real sense they add value to products.

Consumers know that it is vaguely absurd to bottle carbonated water in France and ship it across the world, yet millions of bottles of such water are drunk each year in America, Australia, Hong Kong and elsewhere. We realise too that paying $30 000 or $40 000 for an imported BMW car is a little irrational when a perfectly adequate domestic model can be purchased for one-third of the price. Yet Perrier and BMW are enormously successful. So the added and apparently intangible values afforded by the brand can in practice become very tangible indeed.

MAINTAINING BRAND VALUES

Brand owners must constantly ensure that the qualities and values of their brands are maintained. They must continue to appeal to the consumer and should be developed so as to maintain their attractiveness in a changing society. In other words, the brand can seldom, except in the short term, shield the brand owner from his own failure to maintain quality, his failure to keep his brand in good repair or even from his own rapaciousness or stupidity.

In the 1960s the British brewing industry, in an attempt to streamline and modernise its activities, made a concerted attempt to change the formulation and presentation of existing branded beers, arguably for the worse. Public outrage was slow to develop but develop it did. Loyalty to many of the leading brands fell considerably and the brewing industry was forced to reverse its policies.

This relative slowness of consumers to desert estbalished brands was demonstrated too in the 1970s when product quality and reliability at Jaguar Cars plummeted. Sales followed the product quality spiral downwards but when a new management restored quality, loyalty to the brand returned.

Brands are therefore fairly robust and capable of surviving in adversity. But consumers are not fools and will not maintain their support for a brand once it ceases to keep its side of the bargain.

BRAND EXTENSION

One of the most difficult decisions facing the owners of existing brands is that of 'extend or not?'. On the one hand, the brand owner foresees the possibility of endowing a new product with some or all the qualities of an existing brand. He can thus enter a market more cheaply, establish his new product more quickly and increase the overall support and exposure of the brand. On the other hand, the brand owner faces the possibility that by extending the brand to cover a new product all he is really doing is diluting the appeal of his existing brand.

In Britain, Cadbury's have, over the years, increasingly extended the Cadbury name to embrace not only chocolate and candy products but such mainstream food products as mashed potatoes, dried milk, soups and beverages. It is arguable that in using the Cadbury name as an endorsement of quality, origin and value on non-chocolate products they have diluted its reputation for excellence and its power in the chocolate area. It could be argued that the Cadbury brand should have been reserved solely for chocolate and candy products and a new brand developed for mainstream food products. Such a new brand would perhaps have taken greater effort and investment to establish in the market-place but it would have preserved the integrity of the existing brand. Carnation's extension of its brand from human foods to petfoods has similarly been seen as potentially diluting the excellence of the original Carnation brand. Furthermore, by developing portfolios of power brands, as opposed to extending a single brand, more ready divestment is possible of activities which have become inappropriate. Also, in situations such as the contamination of Tylenol, it ensures that potential damage is contained and does not extend to a wide number of products.

Alternatively, brand extension has proved in many cases to be a remarkably successful strategy – it has reduced the risk and cost of new product entries, increased the exposure of brands and made brands more attractive and contemporary to consumers. Chanel, for example, have introduced ranges of male fragrances under what was exclusively a feminine brand without the slightest dilution of the existing brand, and with the new product ranges assuming all the desired attributes of the original. Certain alcoholic beverage manufacturers – for example, Cinzano – have successfully and profitably applied their brand names to products completely outside their mainstream business – in Cinzano's case to clothing. Anheuser-Busch have successfully extended their brand and applied it to a high quality range of snack products. It is apparent, therefore, that brand extension is entirely practical but needs to be treated with considerable care and skill. Certainly the wild enthusiasm for brand extension shown in the early 1980s is misplaced and likely to prove harmful.

What then are the factors which should govern our decisions in this area? A wide number of techniques exist for producing brand inventories, for market testing and mapping and for concept development. Ultimately, a brand owner has to take a long hard look at his brand and say, 'What is it?', 'What reasonably could it become?' and 'What do I want it to become?'

What does the Lea and Perrins brand represent? An ability to enhance foods? Sauces in general? Excellence in savoury sauces? Traditional food values? Olde England? Cocktail mixers? Could the Lea and Perrins brand be extended to embrace other savoury sauces? Possibly. To embrace dessert sauces? Probably not. (Lea and Perrins strawberry-flavoured ice cream topping! Ugh!) To embrace certain foods? Possibly (e.g. Lea and Perrin's traditional steak and kidney pie).

What does the Marlboro brand represent? Excellence in cigarettes? Style and sophistication? The modern male? Could we envisage a range of Marlboro smoker's requisites? Yes – in fact these are already on sale. Marlboro cheroots? Just possible but unlikely. Marlboro sports clothing? Yes – it is already on sale. Marlboro light scotch? Possibly. Marlboro stout? Probably not. Marlboro cocktail snacks? Possibly yes. Marlboro doughnuts? Probably no.

Which, of course, all seems perfectly logical and sensible. Yet a leading savoury sauce manufacturer did introduce under its brand name a range of ice cream toppings – it was a disaster. Rolls-Royce did supply car engines to a manufacturer of limousines selling at one-third of the Rolls-Royce price and allowed their brand name to be used in the promotion of these cut-price limos.

So the moral in brand extension is to act with great caution and remember that it may not be extension at all – simply dilution. But if you do decide to go ahead look at your brand very carefully. Consider the qualities of real value to the consumer – and these may not be immediately obvious. Look too at opportunities outside your normal sphere of activities – a cigarette manufacturer does not need to manufacture clothing to derive an attractive income from activities in the clothing area.

OWN LABEL

Producers of branded goods and retailers necessarily live together in a state of mild mutual tension. The manufacturer needs the retailer in order to market his brands yet wants to control margins, selling prices, volumes, how far his brand is discounted, where it is displayed, how it is displayed, the breadth of the range stocked, and so on. The retailer, on the other hand, wants to be able to shop the market for the products he sells, determine his own selling prices, arrange his own store layout and be free, when it suits him, of pressures from the brand owner.

The brand owner, therefore, frequently feels that the retailer is destroying his brands and failing to appreciate their inherent values. The retailer often accuses the brand owner of failing to support his brands, of overvaluing them and of other similar misdemeanours.

But in the end the brand owner and the retailer generally need each other and usually compromise. But not always. One option open to the retailer is to develop his own brands and this most major retailers do. Such 'own brands', besides offering benefits to the consumer, serve as a sort of warning to the brand owner by the retailer that perhaps he is not essential. Also, as the manufacture of 'own brand' products is often undertaken by companies with spare manufacturing capacity on a marginal or quasi-marginal basis, they are frequently cheaper and can be used by retailers to attract customers and to establish price points in their negotiations with brand owners.

Thus conventional 'own brands' are the tactical weapons of the retailer. In so far as such brands embrace common sets of product attributes, even if they are 'no name' brands in white boxes, they are every bit as much brands as are manufacturer's.

Own-branding has been taken very much further than this by certain retailers. In Britain, for example, the corporate name Marks and Spencer and the product brand St Michael have come to represent excellence, quality and value across a very wide range of clothing products, household textiles, foodstuffs, toys, and so on. Marks and Spencer only sell 'own brand' merchandise. They specify what they require, conduct their own market testing (normally simply by putting products on to the shelf in a few stores to see if they sell) and exercise tight quality control. Their products could be accused at times of lacking 'intangible brand values' and consumers complain that if they buy a garment from Marks and Spencer they are likely to see hundreds of the identical garments within a few weeks. Nonetheless, it is evident that the brands Marks and Spencer and St Michael have enormous appeal in Britain.

Perhaps the ultimate example of the appeal of 'own brands' is the Harrods brand. Harrods have allowed cigarette and other manufacturers to produce goods under their name for sale through other retail outlets. Thus the 'own brand' has come full circle and become a manufacturer brand, albeit on a licensed basis.

It is important then when considering 'own brands' to see them not as an alternative to branding but rather as a different way of using branding, in this case by retailers.

THE LIFE-CYCLE OF A BRAND

In practical terms most brands need have no life-cycle at all. Such major world power brands as Kodak, Coca-Cola, Goodyear, Hoover, Gillette, Schweppes and IBM have been with us for generations and are all still thriving and enormously successful. Indeed, it is the potentiality of such long life which makes new brand development so exciting and important, and existing successful brands so valuable.

But like anything else, brands only survive if they are looked after. If Kodak had stopped product development and innovation with the Box Brownie, the Kodak brand would have been of interest only to historians; if Coca-Cola had not continued to promote and support the brand, or had allowed it to become a generic name like sarsaparilla or soda rather than a proprietary trademark, it too would not be in such powerful use today.

The potentially indefinite life of a brand is recognised in law. Whereas patents have a finite life of, generally, fifteen to twenty years and then expire (indeed, once a product is patented it may take many years to get to market so the practical market life of a patent may be only a few years) registered trademarks, if properly maintained and renewed, can go on indefinitely.

INTERNATIONAL BRANDING

Another important characteristic of most major brands is that they are international in scope – Charlie is as likely to appeal in Brazil as in Hong Kong. The developed countries, whose inhabitants are the major consumers of branded goods, have shown in this century an enormous 'coming together' of consumer tastes and expectations. Regional and local tastes, attitudes and preferences remain and these must be taken into consideration. Nonetheless, brands which are successful in one market are increasingly likely to have appeal to consumers on an international basis.

The reasons for this are many and include improved communications, increased travel and greater language tuition in schools (particularly of English). The most important reason, however, is that wherever we live, whatever our colour and whatever our culture we are all very much the same. Coca-Cola tastes as good to a teenager in Kowloon as in Chippewa Falls, Wisconsin. A couple in Tokyo take as much pleasure in looking at their Kodak wedding photographs as a couple in Nairobi. Wherever we live and whatever our background we will respond to well-produced, attractive branded products.

The possibility of developing new international brands rather than simply national brands is an appealing one to brand owners. International brands are reassuring to consumers, take advantage of the enormous and growing promotional overlap between countries brought about by travel, sports sponsorship, satellite TV, and so on. They also give brand owners substantial economies in such areas as production, inventory and promotion – one excellent TV commercial for the whole of Europe adapted to suit local conditions and languages might cost $150 000; twelve skimped locally made commercials could easily cost in total a million dollars.

Most importantly, international brands provide companies with a coherence to their international activities. International companies which permit, or are forced to accept, a proliferation of local brands often find a fragmentation of their activities. In theory each of these brands should be more ideally adapted to particular local conditions; in practice the appeal, coherence and power of competitive international brands makes it difficult for the local brands to compete.

DEVELOPING NEW BRANDS

Successful brands, whether they are national or international, offer consumers something of value which is different from that offered by competitive brands, and which they are prepared to purchase. Once satisfied they will continue to purchase until their needs change, the brand changes or they are offered a product which better suits their requirements.

What are the implications of this? Surely that in developing new brands one should seek those which are meaningfully differentiated from competitive products, which afford the consumer a reason to change, will continue to meet his requirements on an ongoing basis and which are difficult to imitate?

In practice, most branding is concerned with products which are relatively undifferentiated in terms of product specification or performance and where consumers are relatively satisfied with existing brands. It would seem logical that, under these circumstances, manufacturers would seek out those components of the brand which are susceptible to innovation and look to create meaningful differences there. Unfortunately, this seldom happens. Take perfumes as an example. In a market environment where all the leading fragrances have exotic French brand names and where a sort of Gallic brand 'soup' exists, why not look at developing a sophisticated Japanese or Indian-style fragrance? Or sell the fragrances only by mail order or through direct sales techniques?

Consider too the market for wine. The cheaper end of the market is characterised by an enormous proliferation of brands all relatively undifferentiated from each other and with no brand enjoying more than a minute share. Is this not a situation similar to that which existed in the nineteenth century with soft drinks? Every American drug store had an ability to concoct for its customers a soft drink to their specifications yet no real assurance existed as to quality or origin. The bottled Coca-Cola brand then provided this assurance. It was differentiated from existing products, appealing to customers and quickly came to dominate the market. Does not a similar opportunity exist in the wine market? Certainly suppliers have tried to develop volume branded wine – Nicolas in France is an example – though so far complete international success has eluded them. But the opportunity remains.

It is estimated that seventeen out of twenty new brands fail. The reasons for failure can sometimes be attributed to product problems, at other times to distribution problems, to changes in legislation, to bad luck or to bad management. Most commonly, however, the reason for failure is simply that the new brands do not offer the consumer anything of interest that he does not have already – they are not differentiated meaningfully from existing products. Most new brands are simply approximate facsimiles of those in existence – they are as close as they can be to existing brands within the constraints imposed by trademark law, passing off, copyright and corporate pride.

Most lagers or light beers have historically been presented in Britain as having a north European heritage but now even such 'genuine' Continental lagers as Heineken and Carlsberg are brewed locally. Brewers seeking new brands have sought the assistance of consumers and they have generally confirmed that, yes, lagers are seen as Continental and not as British. The result has been that brewers have launched a mass of 'pseudobrau' brands festooned with Gothic lettering, German eagles, -brau suffixes and umlauts. The brand owners have believed that they are giving the consumer what he wants. In fact they have simply created a salad of relatively undifferentiated brands most of which the consumer recognises as being phoney.

Why is it that organisations constantly launch new brands which are banal and imitative, which are initially supported by heavy advertising, coupons, giveaways and sweepstakes but which once such support is removed, disappear into obscurity? The reason is partly that research tends to push in this direction. After all, when seeking the views and opinions of consumers these tend to be formed by their current terms of reference. The manufacturer is advised that if he wants a successful new brand it should possess the qualities of the existing market leader.

Another factor is simple risk avoidance. By imitating an existing brand or brands the new brand can be shown as being not too far wrong, even if it proves a failure! Lack of imagination also plays a part. Brand owners as well as consumers are subject to the influences of the existing brand culture and find it difficult to think beyond that culture. Equally important, however, is a genuine wish on the part of manufacturers to imitate directly successful competitive brands. Today's consumer markets are tough and rugged. Competition is fierce. The urge to tackle competition head-on in their territory is a real one even if it might be more sensible to avoid a set-piece battle and take on the opponents on one's own ground, or develop completely new weapons or even revert to guerilla tactics.

Some brand owners, however, deliberately set themselves up to appeal to the myopic shopper, the shopper who recognises products by generalised shape or colour (in Britain all bottles of tonic have yellow labels, soda black and white labels, ginger ale brown and green labels, and so on). Perhaps the major exponents of this art are the retailers. If the leading manufacturer's brand of Continental-style instant coffee has a gold cap and a gold label, so too will the 'own brand'. If the leading dog food brand has a blue label and a picture of a Mongolian elk hound, the own-label product will have a blue label and a Manchurian elk hound. Though such 'own branding' by retailers at times barely stops short of 'passing-off', the natural reluctance of manufacturers to face up to their major customers, the retailers, on this matter has led to such practices becoming at times virtually standard.

But the remedy to dull, imitative 'me too' brands is not generally extreme novelty and wild innovation. Indeed, opportunities seldom exist to do this even if one wished to. Rather, anyone developing a new brand must look at the components of the brand and its totality, and ask 'why should anyone buy this?', 'what am I offering that existing products don't?' If credible answers cannot be found to these questions the brand is unlikely to succeed.

The corollary of this is that when you have a new product with a more than average measure of innovation be sure not to conceal its novelty by developing a brand personality similar to other, less innovative products. For example, to call a new savings plan Supa-Save when it takes advantage of new legislation in a novel way and when there are thousands of existing conventional 8 per cent, 8.5 per cent, 9.25 per cent, 9.5 per cent and 9.75 per cent Supa-Saves is clearly absurd – the novel, exciting product is projected as being just another brand of savings plan. But be sure – this happens all the time. Furthermore, and despite the established wisdom, consumers do not in fact work hard to track down better mouse traps.

It is also inappropriate when branding an innovative product to develop a brand personality which is easy for competition to copy. The innovator simply takes all the risks of innovation and, once successful, is swamped by a mass of similar brands. Yet this too happens frequently – a descriptive and unprotectable brand name is used or a conventional packaging style adopted which encourages ready imitation.

Innovative, differentiated brands can also have a further potent advantage. Not only can they offer the consumer real benefits and thus give the consumer a reason to change from an existing brand, they can also serve to outmode existing brands. The new one not only offers the consumer a new set of values, it wrong-foots the opposition and shows it up as being unexciting and staid. In the 1950s, in Britain, the culture of car branding was largely 'British' in style – cars had names like Westminster, Prefect, Herald and Oxford. Ford then introduced the Cortina. The post-war boom was getting under way, consumers were starting to take organised Mediterranean holidays and Britain's earlier insularity was beginning to dissolve. Cortina hit the mood of the moment. It was fresh, exciting, different and a little foreign and sophisticated. Not only did the brand name assist in positioning the new car in an interesting and fresh fashion, it also wrong-footed competitive products and made them look somewhat dull and old-fashioned.

CONCLUSIONS

Branding is a creative process. It uses research techniques and the skills of a number of specialists. But in the end it is about creating distinctiveness – in a consumer relevant fashion. Unfortunately, most branding seems to be concerned not with distinctiveness but with sameness, with camouflaging the brand so that it melds in among all the other brands on the market. To be distinctive, to refuse to follow the herd takes courage – and it can be highly rewarded.

2 History of Branding

ADRIAN ROOM

BEGINNINGS

The history of branding can be traced back for many centuries before the term came to acquire its modern usage. In Greek and Roman times – and even before that – there were various ways of promoting wares or goods, whether they were wines or pots, metals or ointments. Messages would be written informing the public that this man, at this address, could make shoes and that the man who lived over there, at that address, was a scribe. The Greeks also used town criers to announce the arrival of ships with particular cargoes.

Much early advertising and marketing (in the literal sense) was thus done on a personal basis with the name of a particular individual as important as that of his product or service. The modern development of this can be seen in the name of the private shopkeeper over his shop and some of the best known chain store names have originated as that of a single shop.

In the earliest days shops, as distinct from individuals, were quick to devise a good method of selling their wares. This was the use of pictures. In Rome, for example, a butcher's shop would display a sign depicting a row of hams (Plate 2.1) while a shoemaker would display a picture of a boot and a dairy would make itself known by a crude sketch of a cow. Such pictorial promotion was a forerunner of the many inn and pub signs with which we in Britain are familiar today (Plate 2.2). In classical times many potential purchasers were illiterate and would be able to identify a particular product only from a picture. Again, in our own time the use of pictorial advertising is exploited in many ingenious ways to accompany a brand name and draw the attention of the public to it. A more sophisticated and literate age has led, too, to the use of visual puns to suggest the brand name concerned: the lance on the Lancia logo, the shell to match Shell, the bird's eye in the Birds Eye logo and the nest and nestlings that illustrate the Nestlé products.

THE GROWTH OF BRANDING

Modern branding and the use of individual brand names has its origin in the nineteenth century. The Industrial Revolution and the consequent development of advertising and marketing techniques made the selection of a good brand name of great importance. In both America and Europe the rapid increase in population, expansion of the railways and construction of new factories, brought with them a keen public demand for a whole range of newly available products, from domestic goods such as home medicines to electrical and mechanical devices. In fact, the greater the quantity and variety of products, the greater became the demand for them and this resulted in the need for manufacturers and marketers to choose a brand name that would be effective in as many ways as possible: memorable, pronounceable, original and, in many instances, directly or indirectly descriptive of the product it denoted. Later, of course, trademark laws were to clarify and impose restrictions on the sorts of names that could be protected – legal protection was not given equally to all types of brand names.

The accompanying list of American leaders in national advertising in the 1890s shows the range and variety of actual brand names that were already beginning to emerge (some of them still well known today) and enables some clear categories to be distinguished. Among them are the following:

(1) Names based on a *personal name*, whether that of the inventor, patentee, shopkeeper or some other person associated with the product, e.g. Baker's Cocoa, Cook's Tours, Edison Phonograph, Hammond Typewriter, Pond's Extract, Postum Cereal (after Charles William Post, who developed it) and Jaeger Underwear.

(2) Names based on a *place name*, often that of the original place where the product was invented, sold or developed, e.g. Columbia Bicycles, New England Mincemeat, Pittsburgh Stogies (a type of stout shoe).

(3) *Invented scientific* names (Plate 2.3), usually based on Latin or Greek (or even both), e.g. Caligraph Typewriter ('beautiful writing'), Cuticura Soap ('skin care'), Gramophone (see below), Sozodont Dentifrice ('tooth saver').

(4) *'Status'* names derived from fine-sounding English words, e.g. Crown Pianos, Diamond Dyes, Gold Dust, Monarch Bicycles, Regal Shoes, Victor Bicycles, Camp Coffee (Plate 2.4).

(5) *'Good association'* names, often ones that have a true or purported story of origin, e.g. Ivory Soap, Quaker Oats, Sunlight Soap, White Label Soups. (All the associations here are of purity and wholesomeness.)

(6) *Artificial* names that may or may not resemble real words, e.g. Kodak (see below), Uneeda Biscuit (slogan: 'Do You Know Uneeda Biscuit?').

(7) *Descriptive* names, e.g. Rambler Bicycle, Shredded Wheat (later to be the subject of legal debate as a trademark).

Some of the names in the selection here would today not be acceptable for registration as trademarks under present trademark laws but the distinctive categories for brand name creation had clearly already been established, and many more recent names can be readily assigned to one of the classes outlined (e.g. Birds Eye to category (1), Bostik to (2) (Boston), Linguaphone to (3), and so on).

Mention has already been made of the use of pictorial advertising to accompany and support a brand name. The degree to which it does so may vary from the direct to the allusive. Many car marque logos were to be similarly indirect and the visual pun or reference not so obvious as in the case of Lancia (Plate 2.5). The Rover logo (Plate 2.6), for example, showed a Viking ship and head (the Vikings were 'sea rovers') and the Volkswagen sported a device that was an oblique reference to its place of manufacture, the town of Wolfsburg (Plate 2.7). The exploitation of a brand name's potential can be extended in other directions, too, such as the famous 'Sch. . . you know who' advertisement and the wide use of apt slogans to suggest a brand name.

THE DEVELOPMENT OF LEADING BRANDS

The need to select a brand name that could be as effective internationally as nationally was a factor that was appreciated early on by companies, and it is interesting to examine the ways in which some of the most famous names originated and to see to what extent they have actually become effective in the many different languages of the world.

Two well-known brand names that were created within a year or two of each other (both in the United States) are Coca-Cola (Plate 2.8) and Kodak. The first of these is a meaningful name (descriptive, as in category (7) above), while the other has no meaning (so is in category (6)).

The name Coca-Cola is based on two of the product's original constituents – extracts from *coca* leaves and from the *cola* nut. That coca leaves also yield cocaine was a factor that did not then, in the 1880s, concern the manufacturers and indeed originally the drink did actually contain minute quantities of the drug. In the early days it was marketed as an 'Esteemed Brain Tonic and Intellectual Beverage'! Sales of the drink grew so rapidly that its name was soon popularly shortened to Coke. Although this was in effect a further reminder of the original cocaine connection, the manufacturers were keen to stake their legal claim to this version of the name, particularly as other companies were now marketing their own versions of the drink under similar names. After a rather complex legal tussle the company succeeded in its claim but not until 1920 when the familiar version of the name had been current for several years. The product is today unique in having two equally well-known brand names, one chiefly used for the international market (Coca-Cola) and the other one mainly adopted by English-speaking consumers (Coke). Both names are, however, of identical legal status in most countries. Even so, the fact that there are now many types of cola drink on the market (the word 'cola' is not a proprietary name) constantly prompts the company to remind the public of the interconnection between the two names. Hence the clever slogan of the mid-1980s – 'Coca-Cola is Coke, Coke is Coca-Cola'.

The name has turned out to be an excellent one for the international market. It is certainly memorable, easy to pronounce and write in different languages (even in non-Roman scripts), and has the incisive 'K' sound that is often chosen for effective international use. It also so happens that the elements comprising the name are internationally comprehensible, since 'coca' and 'kola' are native words and have been adopted by most major languages in an unaltered form.

Kodak is a similarly successful name worldwide and also has the two effective 'Ks'. However, unlike Coca-Cola, it is meaningless, but we are fortunate enough to have on record the account of the man who created it, explaining how he arrived at the final form. This gives an important insight into the thinking behind an 'artificial' name, and one that is historic by branding standards.

The creator of the name was the photographic pioneer George Eastman, who registered it on 4 September 1888. His account of the creation is as follows:

> I knew a trade name must be short, vigorous, incapable of being misspelled to an extent that will destroy its identity and, in order to satisfy trademark laws, it must mean nothing. The letter K had been a favourite with me – it seemed a strong, incisive sort of letter. Therefore, the word I wanted had to start with K. Then it became a question of trying out a great number of combinations of letters that made words starting and ending with K. The word Kodak is the result.

The name became so popular that, like Coca-Cola, it nearly became generic for 'camera' in some countries, and countermeasures had to be taken to prevent this. The generic adoption of a trade name is, of course, not simply a tribute to its success but also a peril inherent in its popularity.

These two names, Coca-Cola and Kodak, were thus established at an early stage worldwide in their originally created form and have retained their prominence today. There can hardly be a single person in any country that has not heard of one or both of these names.

Sometimes, for legal or other reasons, a brand name will appear in different forms, and sometimes the same product is marketed in different countries under entirely different names. A case in point is that of Esso. The name originated from the initials (SO) of the Standard Oil Company of New Jersey which was set up as the chief company of Rockefeller's Oil Trust in 1888. When the Trust split up, however, Standard Oil was obliged to look for another name in those American states where newly formed companies were trading as a result of the dissolution of the Trust. Finally Esso decided it wished to revert to the use of a single brand name and, after extensive tests and surveys Exxon was found to be the most easily recognised and protectable name – its distinctive double X makes it memorable and easy to write. The name also, of course, hints at the Esso of the original.

It is probably no coincidence that all three names considered above, Coca-Cola, Kodak and Exxon, are all phonetically distinctive and incisive and this characteristic signifies many well-known brand names (other examples are Kleenex, Cuticura, Klaxon and Kotex).

THE DEATH OF A BRAND

An interesting example of a brand name that has changed several times, finally losing its legal status as a proprietary name in Britain and some other countries, is Gramophone – an 'invented scientific' name. The first Gramophone was patented by Emile Berliner in Washington DC on 8 November 1887. Berliner chose the name to differentiate his instrument from its predecessors (his machine used discs and earlier machines had used a cylinder). He devised the name by reversing the two elements of Phonogram, an instrument which itself had a name based on Phonograph ('sound writing'). This last name (historically the first) later became generic in America as Gramophone did in Britain. One company setting up to manufacture the instrument in the United States devised a further name based on it, Graphophone, for its own models. Meanwhile, in Britain The Gramophone Company was established. Yet another version of the instrument emerged in America as the Victrola (originally the Victor). This profusion of related names and instruments led to Gramophone or Phonograph (or a similar spelling to suit national languages) being adopted as the generic name for the machine in many countries. In Russia, however, the initial name of Grammofon (borrowed from the German Grammophon) was superseded by Patefon when a new model of the instrument with a permanent sapphire needle was introduced in the early twentieth century. This came from the surname of the French inventor Emile Pathé, brother of Charles Pathé who founded the famous film company.

SOME WELL-KNOWN BRANDS

The names of man-made fibres comprise a special category of brand names since the word nylon, on which many of them are based, is not a proprietary name. It was devised by the Du Pont company in 1938 as a generic name and was itself based on the earlier name rayon. This is also a generic name and was devised by the National Retail Drygoods Association in 1924 from the word ray. Various other names based on the word nylon, most of which are registered trademarks, have been adopted in other countries – for example, Crepon in France and Dederon in East Germany.

It is significant that many brand names that have come to be known worldwide are either scientific in origin or easily memorable in different languages. Among the scientific names containing classical elements are Aspirin (now generic in Britain and some other countries), based on the German equivalent of '*a*cetylated *spir*aeic acid', Cellophane (generic in the United States but still a registered trademark elsewhere), Frigidaire, Klaxon (based on the Greek word meaning 'I will make a loud noise'), Linguaphone, Thermos (generic in the United States since 1963 but still a keenly protected registered trademark elsewhere) and Vaseline, based on the German for water and the Greek for oil. Among short, memorable international brand names are Berec (the initials of British Ever Ready Electrical Company), Bic (pioneered by the Frenchman Marcel Bich), Biro (invented by the Hungarian László Biró), Decca (of uncertain origin, but said by some to represent musical notes), Jeep (from a cartoon character that made a sound 'jeep', but later associated with the initials of 'general purpose') and Xerox (based ultimately on the Greek word for dry). These names are internationally known because the products themselves have been successfully marketed in different countries.

The most obvious examples of truly international names, however, are those of cars which are exported worldwide and, even more, those of airlines which are international in the literal sense of the word. Some, understandably, have developed as abbreviations or acronyms of the original name, so that today worldwide recognition has been gained by such names as Pan-Am (Pan American World Airways, founded in 1927), Qantas (Queensland and Northern Territory Aerial Service, founded in 1920), and Sabena (Société Anonyme Belge d'Exploitation de la Navigation Aérienne, set up in 1923).

THE UNIQUENESS OF BRAND NAMES

What makes all such well-known brand names unique is that they are among the only words in the language to have been deliberately created, even when based on existing names. They did not develop naturally as personal names and place names have done. Moreover, although very familiar to most people, they are relatively young. Personal and place names often date back hundreds of years. Brand names, on the other hand, started to develop little more than a century ago and many of them have been in existence for a much shorter time than that. Meanwhile, the creation of new brand names continues, and although methods of devising and selecting them are infinitely more sophisticated today than at any previous time, the basic principles and categories established in the nineteenth century still hold good.

LEADERS IN AMERICAN ADVERTISING IN THE 1890s

Adams Tutti Frutti Gum
Aeolian Company
American Express Traveller's
  Cheques
Armour Beef Extract
Autoharp

Baker's Cocoa
Battle Ax Plug Tobacco
Beardsley's Shredded Codfish
Beeman's Pepsin Gum
Bent's Crown Piano
Burlington Railroad
Burnett's Extracts

California Fig Syrup
Caligraph Typewriter
Castoria
Chicago Great Western
Chicago, Milwaukee & St Paul
  Railroad
Chocolat-Menier
Columbia Bicycles
Cook's Tours
Cottolene Shortening
Crown Pianos
Cuticura Soap

De Long Hook and Eye
Diamond Dyes
Dixon's Graphite Paint
Dixon's Pencils

Edison Phonograph
Epps's Cocoa
Estey Organ

Fall River Line

Felt & Tarrant Comptometer
Ferry's Seeds
Fisher Piano
Fowler Bicycles
Franco American Soup

Garland Stoves
Gold Dust Washing Powder
Gorham's Silver
Gramophone
Great Northern Railroad

Hamburg American Line
Hammond Typewriter
Hartford Bicycle
Hartshorn's Shade Rollers
Heinz's Baked Beans
Hires' Root Beer
Hoffman House Cigars
Huyler's Chocolates

Ingersoll Watches
Ives & Pond Piano
Ivory Soap

Jaeger Underwear

Kirk's American Family Soap
Kodak

Liebig's Extract of Beef
Lipton's Teas
Lowney's Chocolates
Lundborg's Perfumes

Mason & Hamlin Piano
Mellin's Food
Mennen's Talcum Powder

Michigan Central Railroad
Monarch Bicycles
Munsing Underwear
Murphy Varnish Company

New England Mincemeat
New York Central Railroad
North German Lloyd

Old Dominion Line
Oneita Knitted Goods

Packer's Tar Soap
Pearline Soap Powder
Pearltop Lamp Chimneys
Pears' Soap
Pettijohn's Breakfast Food
Pittsburgh Stogies
Pond's Extract
Postum Cereal
Prudential Insurance Co

Quaker Oats

Rambler Bicycles
Redfern Corsets
Regal Shoes
Remington Typewriter
Rising Sun Stove Polish
Rogers 1847 Silverware
Royal Baking Powder

Santa Fe Railroad
Sapolio
Scott's Emulsion
Sears, Roebuck & Co
Sen Sen For The Breath

Shredded Wheat
Smith Premier Typewriter
Sorosis Shoes
Southern Railway
Sozodont Dentifrice
Spalding Bicycles
Spencerian Pens
Standard Mfg. Co. Bathtubs
Steinway Piano
Sterling Bicycles
Studebaker Carriages
Sunlight Soap

Uneeda Biscuit
Union Pacific Railroad

Van Camp's Pork & Beans
Van Houten's Cocoa
Vaughan's Seeds
Vichy Celestins
Victor Bicycles
Vin Mariani
Vose Piano

Waltham Watches
Warner's Corsets
Warwick Cycles
Waterbury Watches
Waterman Fountain Pen
Waverley Bicycles
Weber Piano
White Label Soups
Whitman's Chocolates
Williams Shaving Soap
Winchester Arms
Woodbury's Facial Soap
Wool Soap

REFERENCES

Arnold, Oren, *What's in a Name: Famous Brand Names* (New York: Julian Messner, 1979).
Button, Henry and Lampert, Andrew, *The Guinness Book of the Business World* (Enfield: Guinness Superlatives, 1976).

Klepner, Otto, *Advertising Procedure*, 8th ed. (Englewood Cliffs: Prentice-Hall, 1983).

Moskowitz, Milton, Katz, Michael, and Levering, Robert (eds) *Everybody's Business: An Almanac* (San Francisco: Harper & Row, 1980).

Nicholson, Tim, *Car Badges of the World* (London: Cassell, 1970).

Presbury, Frank, *The History and Development of Advertising* (New York: Doubleday, Doran & Co., 1929).

Room, Adrian, *Dictionary of Trade Name Origins*, rev. ed. (London: Routledge & Kegan Paul, 1983).

Stiling, Marjorie, *Famous Brand Names, Emblems and Trade-Marks* (Newton Abbot: David & Charles, 1980).

UK Trade Names, 8th ed. (East Grinstead: Kompass Publishers, 1984).

3 The Psychology of Names

LESLIE COLLINS

WHAT IS A NAME?

A name is a simple thing; it is a label – although there is also an element of mystery and magic about it. If we give a name to something which did not have one before it is like bringing that thing into existence for the first time. It seems to add an extra dimension to anything if we give it a name. A name is also capable, with familiarity and repetition, of being a kind of incantation.

Philosophers have often puzzled over the idea of names. What puzzled Plato is that there may be one common name, like 'table' or 'chair' – but an infinite variety of actual chairs. There are big and small chairs; some have arms, some don't; there are three-legged chairs, four-legged chairs, rocking chairs, and so on. And when you see a chair which is quite unlike any other you have seen before, there is no difficulty in recognising it and calling it a chair.

Plato recognised this phenomenon – this gift of language we have, this sure touch in using names – and he felt it needed explaining. So he supposed there must be a kind of Ideal Chair in Heaven, which in some sense we know about, or have seen, and which enables us to recognise and correctly name all the variety of chairs we meet in life. Sir John Wolfenden, who was a student of the classics, called this idea of Plato's 'the Celestial Warehouse theory'.

Finding names for things is not limited to the world of marketing as we know it. For example, people have to think of names for radio and television programmes – 'Panorama', 'Sixty Minutes', 'Kojak', 'Dynasty', 'The Living World'. Authors have to think of names for characters and books, they have their *Goldfinger*, *Cat on a Hot Tin Roof*, *Little Drummer Boy*, *Passage to India*, *Megatrends*.

What does the name 'Norma Baker' suggest to you? Or 'Harry Webb'? Or 'Sam Goldfish'? Or 'Alice Marks'? Or 'Maurice Micklewhite'? Well, Norma Baker is better known as Marilyn Monroe; Harry Webb as Cliff Richard; Sam Goldfish as Sam Goldwyn; Alice Marks as Alicia Markova! Some people change their names. In George Orwell's nightmare *1984*, people were deprived of any name, and suffered the ignominy of just being numbers. Notice the word 'ignominy'. It originally meant 'without a name' but it has come to imply

22

something unworthy. In contrast to this we speak of a person's making a name for himself usually to mean achieving greater esteem. We speak of 'adding lustre to a name'. A title in the Honours List is a literal reflection of that: a title embellishes a name or even changes it in a way that is intended to render the person named as more honourable. Not only does a change of name represent upgrading of the thing named, but some name changing is itself aspirant. Hence a rat-catcher becomes a rodent operative, a dustman a refuse collector, a bookie a turf accountant. The *Daily Telegraph* recently reported a gem of such aspirant renaming. A used-car salesman in South London has been reported as describing himself as a 'Pre-owned vehicle re-allocation consultant'!

What about names of places? Would you rather live in Crouch End or Potters Bar? In Paramus or San Francisco? In Knightsbridge or Neasden? In the Bronx or Boston? In Durham or Scunthorpe? In Hollywood Beach or Palm Beach? You can feel the incantational 'throb' or vibration there is in names.

Again, people give names to their pets, their houses; names have to be found for hotels, pubs and restaurants; for streets, new towns – even for hurricanes.

Anyone who is a parent will have been involved, in some way, in the process of giving a name to a human being. You may name your son Simon or Cedric, your daughter Jane or Jemima. For the name you give your child reflects something of your basic attitude towards it, and since a child responds to parental attitudes he or she will be a different person according to his or her name. Giving a name to a child is different from finding a brand name since the new child's name does not have to be unique and novel. There are fashions in first names and children are often named after older relatives which emphasises affinity and continuity.

The fact that we are able to give names to things, some of them completely new names, tells us something about language. Animals have systems of communication: as we know, bees communicate with each other by what has been called dance movements; chimpanzees have a range of vocal and other communications. But animal language – if you can call it language – is a practically closed system. They do not generate new symbols, while human language is virtually infinite in possibility: especially when it becomes a written language, and then it takes off into orbit, as far as range is concerned. It is relevant to note, too, that vocal forms, syllables, consonants, vowels, are *not* bound to any particular meaning forms. You can almost do what you like and associate any sound with any meaning.

Or can you?

THE JULIET PRINCIPLE

Shakespeare's much quoted line, spoken by Juliet, runs: 'that which we call a rose, by any other name would smell as sweet'. It suggests that the verbal form 'rose' does not matter; it is what we have come to associate with that verbal form that determines the meaning of the name. I will give the quotation in full because the rest of it makes the point even better. The plot of 'Romeo and Juliet' hinges on the fact that the two lovers come from rival families – the Montagues and Capulets – who have a long-standing fued, each hating the name of the other. Juliet is trying to get round this fact, saying names do not matter:

> Tis but thy name, that is my enemy;
> Thou art thyself though, not a Montague.
> What's Montague? it is nor hand, nor foot,
> Nor arm, nor face, nor any other part
> Belonging to a man. O, be some other name!
> What's in a name? that which we call a rose,
> By any other name would smell as sweet;
> So Romeo would, were he not Romeo call'd,
> Retain that dear perfection which he owes,
> Without that title: – Romeo, doff they name;
> And for that name, which is no part of thee,
> Take all myself.'

There is certainly much to be said in favour of the Juliet approach. Just consider how a sandwich got its name, or a cardigan, or wellingtons. They were named after people, after members of the English nobility. In fact: the 4th Earl of Sandwich, Lord Cardigan, and the Iron Duke, respectively. If these noblemen had been associated with different things, we might well today be eating cardigans, wearing sandwiches on our feet, and having wellingtons knitted for us. And we would think there was nothing remarkable in it at all.

When you think about it, Cadbury and Guinness are family names. If Mr Cadbury had been a brewer and Mr Guinness a confectioner, we might today be drinking Cadbury's stout and eating Guinness chocolate. The fact that the thought is so unpalatable is emphatic justification of the Juliet principle.

On the other hand, supposing the Cadbury family name had been different, had been, shall we say, Mudd (which is an English surname), might he have been tempted to sell his chocolate under a different name?

PHONETIC SYMBOLISM: THE JOYCE PRINCIPLE

There are, however, one or two experiments which run counter to the Juliet principle. Let us call the counter principle the Joyce principle after James Joyce who, in works like *Finnegan's Wake*, depended upon phonetic symbolism as opposed to actual words in order to communicate. The Juliet principle says, 'A rose by any other name'; the Joyce principle would say, 'A rose is a rose is a rose'.

As long ago as 1928, Edward Sapir, a psychologist at the University of Chicago, published a paper entitled 'A Study in Phonetic Symbolism'. This was probably the first paper on the subject. He was interested in aspects of language – nothing to do with commerce or marketing – and he devised an experiment to show that word forms do have a symbolic force of their own, quite apart from referring to any particular object.

He acknowledged that a great part of the language is purely referential. That is to say, certain words derive their functional significance by being associated with particular objects. This association is quite arbitrary and conventional and has grown up historically, its origin lost in the mist of time. Thus the word 'book' refers to an object like this (a book). The association is purely conventional and arbitrary. There is nothing inherent in the term 'book' which implies that it has to be used for that purpose, not is there anything about a book which dictates that it must be referred to by that term. This follows on the same lines as the previous comments on sandwiches and cardigans.

Having said that it does seem, for some reason, that word forms have another level or stratum of meaning – a symbolic level.

Sapir took pairs of meaningless word forms, such as 'mal' and 'mil', which are identical except for the vowel sound. He told his subjects – the people he persuaded to act as guinea pigs in his experiment – that *mal* and *mil* meant 'table' (in an unspecified language). One of these words meant 'large table' and the other 'small table'. The subjects were then asked to indicate which of the words they thought would be the large table and which would be the small. He used sixty such word pairs and all were given arbitrary meanings (table, or something else). All sixty were unlike any real words.

The result of the experiment was that 80 per cent of the time the words with the 'a' sound (he used a long 'ah') were found to indicate the larger object, and the 'i' sound to indicate the smaller object. In other words, quite apart from any actual word or object, the 'a' sound is likely to imply something large, and the 'i' something small. These sounds have a feeling-significance and a certain meaning in themselves.

To make a more watertight test, he repeated the experiment using 100 word pairs and every type of phonetic contrast, that is, not just 'a' and 'i' but forms of a, e, i, o, u and consonants as well, arranged in a random way so that subjects would not realise the object of the test. He used no less than 500 subjects in this experiment ranging from eleven years old to adults.

It is not necessary to go into the details of the experiment here. Suffice it to say that a consistent pattern emerged in the response of the subjects, showing that in the majority of cases they all found the same symbolic value in the word forms, as these suggested large or small, in varying degrees (i.e. the contrast in

'size' connotation between 'a' and 'i' was greater than between 'e' and 'i', etc.).

Sapir concluded that he was encountering an independent psychological factor which he termed 'phonetic symbolism': certain vowels and consonants 'sound bigger' than others.

Now it may be that if you were to amass a large number of words meaning large and another group meaning small, as from a thesaurus, there might be a preponderance of one kind of vowels and consonants in the one, and other kinds of vowels and consonants in the other. The experiment in this case suggested a quite different explanation. It is that acoustically 'large' vowels/ consonants sound larger. Equally, and in addition perhaps, he suggested there could be a kinaesthetic explanation, that in mouthing these words the tongue and mouth position is larger for the 'large' sounds and smaller for the 'small' (cf. 'a' and 'i' respectively). The idea is that a spatially extended mouth movement unwittingly symbolises a larger object.

These hypotheses sound very simple and basic, but in so far as there is such a thing as phonetic symbolism, it could well arise from such a basic origin. In talking to his subjects afterwards, Sapir got the impression that with some the acoustic interpretation fitted better, with others, the kinaesthetic.

Similar experiments were conducted by Stanley Newmann, in which more elaborate statistical methods were used to discriminate between the symbolic values put on different sounds, both vowels and consonants. He felt that he confirmed more tellingly from this data that the symbolic value accorded to sound is 'mechanical' depending on the resonance and articulation of given sounds (i.e. the acoustic and kinaesthetic bases).

He also experimented with a dark and light value, in addition to large and small. He felt he was able to relate light and dark values to aspects of articulation, in a way comparable to that for large and small symbolism.

Newmann did one further thing. He set out to discover whether the symbolic values his subjects attached to certain sounds would be reflected in normal English words. A great number of words relating to size were taken from *Roget's Thesaurus* and separated into those denoting 'large' in various ways and those denoting 'littleness'.

These two lists were analysed for their sound content and compared. The results indicate that the phonetic content of English words takes no account of magnitude, symbolically. Table 3.1 shows, in terms of the indices used, that there is virtually no difference between large and small words as to their phonetic content, taking them as a whole.

However a comparable exercise in the French language suggests that phonetic symbolism *is* reflected in the ordinary vocabulary (see Table 3.2 below). This suggests that phonetic symbolism may be a feature of some languages and not of others. Probably the content of English has been more eclectically formed than that of French.

In a way phonetic symbolism is like onomatopoeia. The word 'splash' suits very well the thing it names by its sound and feel. Onomatopoeia is obvious in

TABLE 3.1   *Relations between phonetic content and meaning, as for largeness and smallness, in the English language*

	Words denoting largeness	Words denoting smallness
1. Long vowels and diphthongs	0.9832	0.9162
2. Consonants	0.8476	0.8024
3. Short vowels	1.3711	1.4072

SOURCE   S. Newmann, 'Further Experiments in Phonetic Symbolism', *Amer. Jnl. Psychol.*, 1933.

TABLE 3.2   *Relation between vowel sounds and concepts in the French vocabulary*

Concepts suggesting	Front vowels	Back vowels
velocity, lightness, nearness	63 p.c.	37 p.c.
slowness, heaviness, distance	33 p.c.	78 p.c.

SOURCE   M. Chastaing, 'Nouvelles Recherches sur le Symbolisme des Voyelles', *Jnl. de Psych.*, 1964.

this respect while most phonetic symbolism is not. Intuitive skill in handling this inherent, unwitting, phonetic symbolism is part of the skill of the copywriter and name creator. It is also, no doubt, part of the art of the poet.

In sum, it appears that phonetic elements of language tend to convey a meaning of their own, a 'feel' of meaning, or symbolic meaning, quite independent of ordinary linguistic meaning. Moreover, this phonetic symbolism is objective, formed in accordance with the mechanical patterns of speech, and age has little effect on it; it is found in children from at least nine years upwards.

JUNG'S WORD ASSOCIATION TEST

The word association test, originally devised by the eminent psychologist Jung, highlights the fact that words have more than simply a referential function. This test was originally used in a clinical setting purportedly as a means of probing the unconscious mind. The procedure is relatively simple: the psychologist has a list of words, mostly quite ordinary words – book, table, chair – but including others that may be emotionally charged for the person being examined and 'planted' among the ordinary words. Such emotionally charged words might be 'mother', 'father', 'husband', 'wife'. The person examined is required to say the first word that comes into his/her mind. Usually the word produced is instantaneous – I say 'table', the patient says 'chair'; I say 'book', the patient says 'pen'; I say 'guilt' . . . Now if there is delay in responding this may itself suggest resistance to disquieting associations that the word has for the individual; and/or the response word produced may signal what the uneasy associations are.

In the commercial field, this process can have an application when trying to link word associations with potential brand names. Various examples can be offered to consumers, inviting them to relate them with each word being considered. This can sometimes yield surprising results. When the word 'lamb' was being evaluated in this way, only 40 per cent associated it with wool, only 10 per cent with food, but 70 per cent with warmth, and 60 per cent with softness. There is another form of the word association procedure where the subject is required to produce as many different associations as possible. This is supposed to be a test of the associative potential of a word. It is probable that a brand name has more potential for penetration and memorability if it is rich in associative possibilities, whereas there are some word forms which are relatively soul-less or anaemic and which promise little magic. The word form 'Whumies' would probably produce a greater network of association than, say, 'Pelatate' or 'Adgel'.

A word list was once compiled, called Glaze's List, which ranked all three-letter word forms according to their inherent associations. No such forms were ever free of any associations. Such a list cannot keep up to date, though, because language moves. Three-letter forms such as 'mod' and 'fab' came into popular usage, and so changed their associative value considerably.

Fernando Dogana considers in greater depth the idea of the suitability or appropriateness of a given brand name, in terms of its phonetic symbolism. He suggests that when a brand name symbolically 'fits' the object that it designates, it seems to have the capacity to represent that object more vividly, more satisfactorily, more satisfyingly, than if it were a less good fit. He cites the fact that workmen, working in a certain quarry in France, use the terms 'pouf', 'paf' and 'pif' to designate three qualities of stone. The first is for the soft quality, paf, the better quality, and pif the hardest, most resistant stone. He suggests that these phonetic variations reflect well the differences in the objects perceived. By contrast, terms like 'hill' and 'mountain' are connected in an arbitrary unsymbolic way to the objects designated.

To the English ear, his 'pouf', 'paf' and 'pif' would seem quite meaningful in the way he suggests. What is of additional interest is that these terms were coined by French-speaking workmen, and Dogana himself wrote his article in Italian. This suggests phonetic symbolism can 'work' with people of different languages.

What makes certain word forms symbolically suitable and able to 'fit' specific objects, more or less satisfactorily? The source of it is partially, as already mentioned, the articulation process of mouthing particular word forms. Dogana seeks to identify, from the field of linguistics, 'meanings' that elements of word formation can symbolise. He gives us suggestions as to how movement, size, shape, luminosity can be conveyed by certain phonetic forms.

Thus, with regard to movement it is said that 'i', 'é', 'è', seem especially apt to express dynamic concepts (rapidity, vivacity, lightness), while the back vowels (a, o, u) are more related to the opposite (slowness, heaviness).

Regarding size, we saw how Sapir with his mal/mil type of contrast found that vowels represent decreasing size as they go in the series a, é, è, i.

As regards shape, acute sounds designate sharp shapes, and flat sounds refer to flat shapes. During one reported experiment subjects were asked to attribute fictitious names (on the Sapir model) to abstract figures, which were either sharp-edged or roundish. The frequency with which vowels were assigned (Table 3.3) clearly shows the sharp and the flat associations.

TABLE 3.3   *Relation of vowel sounds and shapes*

Vowels	Sharp-edged figures	Roundish figures
i	325	7
e	31	46
a	8	71
u	5	118
o	12	141

SOURCE   Ohwahi and Sato, 'Psychological Relationship between Visual and Auditory Stimuli', *Tohuku Psychol. Folio*, 1954.

One investigator noted that an eighteen-month-old child called all round and rolling objects 'golloh' where the rolling articulation seemed to represent the object and movement in question. According to another investigator, quoted by Dogana, degree of *luminosity* is evoked as follows: light is symbolised by 'clear' vowels (i, é, è) while night is characterised by dark vowels (a, o, u).

Newmann claimed, by the statistical treatment of his data, to be able to rank consonants as to the degree to which they suggest darkness or light (Table 3.4).

TABLE 3.4   *Relation between consonants and luminosity*

Decreasing from K to BR		
K .0000	J .4197	GL.7780
S .0000	N .5413	D .8590
L .0151	G .5545	M .9778
H .3159	B .5573	GR1.0438
P .3395	R .6016	BR1.0816

SOURCE   'Further Experiments in Phonetic Symbolism', *American Journal of Psychology*, 1933.

Dogana claims, in general, that psycholinguistic studies show that when we hear a new and unknown word for the first time, it is not neutral but embodies certain resonances and values, caused by the phonetic composition of the word. If you have ever played the dictionary game, known on British television as 'Call my Bluff', you will know that there is a strong tendency to define unknown words in terms of the various kinds of resonances – be it semantic, phonetic, Jungian – that they have.

Dogana further claims that, hearing an unknown name for the first time, whether of a person or a brand, leaves us with a positive or negative first impression and that the 'wrong' naming of a brand can be an enduring handicap. Presumably this view is shared by the people in show business who were responsible for changing the name of Norma Baker to Marilyn Monroe or of Maurice Micklewhite to Michael Caine.

Dogana suggests brand names can be divided into four main categories:

(1) Invented names with no particular expressive value (Omo could be an example).
(2) Invented names having a phonetically symbolic value (e.g. Soflan, to suggest gentleness in a woollen material).
(3) Names having a known semantic significance (e.g. Dual, Mars).
(4) Names with both a semantic and an expressive value (e.g. Crunchie).

He considers the last category, which unites the semantic and the symbolic, to be the most satisfactory brand names.

He offers advice which might help towards creating such names. The recommended steps are:

(1) Identify the qualities or aura of the product that it is intended the name should convey.
(2) Identify word characteristics most apt to reflect these qualities.
(3) Create lists of names by means of various combinations.
(4) Reduce to a short-list and conduct consumer research to determine the most suitable names.

CONCLUSIONS

Names are made of single syllables, or connected syllables. These syllables are never 'neutral', never devoid of meaning or values. Indeed any given name may represent a wealth of meanings, whether referential, symbolic, associative, or combinations of these. That is part of the seemingly infinite resource of language.

The derivation of effective brand names is, among other things, an exercise in the skill and art of using language and, within its own context, is all of a piece with literary creativity generally.

REFERENCES

Chastaing, M., 'Nouvelles Recherches sur le Symbolisme des Voyelles', *Journal de Psychologie*, 1964.
Dogana, Fernando, Psycholinguistic Contributions to the Problem of Brand Names'. Translated from the Italian, for *European Marketing Research Review*, 1967, vol. 11, no. 1, pp. 50–8.
Newmann, S., 'Further experiments in Phonetic Symbolism', *American Journal of Psychology*, 1933.
Sapir, E., 'A study in Phonetic Symbolism', *Journal of Experimental Psychology*, 1929.

4 The Legal Side of Branding

CLARKE GRAHAM
MARK PEROFF

WHAT IS A TRADEMARK?

A trademark is a sign or symbol which distinguishes the goods or services provided by an enterprise. It can consist of a word or words, letters, numbers, symbols, emblems, monograms, signatures, colours or combinations of colours. It can even, in some cases, be a phrase or slogan but whatever it is, it can only properly fulfil its function from both legal and marketing standpoints if it is distinctive. A trademark has three functions:

— to distinguish the goods or services of the enterprise from those of another;
— to indicate the source or origin of the goods or services;
— to represent the goodwill of the trademark owner and to serve as an indication of the quality of his goods or services.

These functions are best expressed by example. The mark Zest is a well-known brand name for soap in the United States. The Zest mark distinguishes one product from the myriad of other soap products on the market. The Zest mark functions as an indication of source. The public recognises that there is a single source for Zest soap – though it may not know what it is. Indeed, under United States trademark practice the actual source of the product does not have to be identified. Finally, the Zest name represents the quality of the product and the goodwill of the manufacturer. A purchaser who is pleased with the first bar of Zest soap he buys will, it is hoped, develop a brand loyalty. He will, when he repurchases soap, look specifically for the Zest brand. Brand loyalty arises from the goodwill which develops in a mark, the direct result of the continued and unvarying quality of the product. It is this brand loyalty which product managers and advertisers continuously seek to develop and to enhance. It is the market share which arises from brand name recognition that in many cases determines the life or death of a consumer product. For this reason, tremendous amounts of money are spent in developing a name, promoting it and protecting it.

Trademarks are, therefore, powerful marketing tools. If well selected, protected and properly used they can help keep the competition at bay, allow the manufacturer to maintain margins and resist the enormous buying power of middlemen or retailers. In effect they allow the manufacturer to talk directly to the consumer and build up in a brand a set of values, both tangible and intangible, which are appropriate and attractive to consumers and conducive to the development of customer loyalty.

WHAT A TRADEMARK IS NOT

Many lay people when talking about brand names will often mistakenly use the terms 'patent', 'copyright' or 'design' when they mean 'trademark'. Though sometimes used by the public interchangeably, these concepts are entirely different and afford distinctly different types of protection.

The protection afforded to patents, copyrights and designs is significantly different from the protection given to trademarks both in its historical and its legal antecedents. The former are limited grants of monopolies awarded by a government to inventors, authors and designers as a reward for their discoveries, their writings and their creative abilities. In the United States, for example, these grants are specifically established by the constitution and have existed since the early days of the nation. Federal statutory trademark protection, on the other hand, did not arise until the late 1800s. The rights attached to patents, copyrights and designs have always been for a limited period of time only. They are not perpetual grants. A trademark, however, may last indefinitely if properly cared for. For example, the trademarks Coca-Cola and Bass are both about one hundred years old.

Trademarks, generally speaking, do not owe their existence to some act of invention, discovery or novelty. They differ too in other respects and since they are often confused with patents, at least terminologically, it is worthwhile giving the following brief description of each of these other forms of monopoly granted under most legal systems:

— Patent protection is concerned with inventions – novel ideas which are capable of industrial exploitation – manufacturing, chemical, packaging processes, etc. The protection for a patented invention is limited, generally, to twenty years.
— Design protection is concerned with features of shape, configuration, pattern or ornamentation of a useful article – the appearance of the product. Provided the features of the design appeal to the eye and are not dictated solely by the function for which the article is intended, the design will be protectable, albeit for a limited period usually fifteen years.

— Copyright is concerned with the physical expression of a creative effort – the law of copyright is designed to prevent the unauthorised copying or reproduction of a person's 'work, labour, skill or taste'. It applies to literary, dramatic, musical and artistic works, sound recordings, film and broadcasting. To enforce a copyright it is necessary to show that the work is original, that the person claiming the copyright is the author of the work (or a successor in title thereto) and that there has been an element of copying. Generally speaking the copyright begins when the work is created and ends fifty years after the death of the author.

Perhaps some of the differences in these rights can best be illustrated by reference to Zest soap, our earlier example. Zest is a trademark of Procter & Gamble. The machines which are used to manufacture Zest soap or the process by which Zest soap is manufactured may be protected by patent. The artwork on the packaging for Zest soap may be protected by copyright. The shape of the container in which the soap is sold or the general appearance of the soap itself may be protected by design.

SELECTING THE TRADEMARK

Role of the Trademark Adviser

In some organisations there is frequently resistance on the marketing side to involving a legal adviser in the trademark selection process – either as a result of sheer ignorance of the legal considerations or because the involvement of a legal adviser is thought of simply as slowing down or detracting from the creative, frontline job the marketing team is doing. Trademark advisers are often seen as having (at times with some justification!) little idea about the marketing considerations involved and their advice is often viewed as simply obstructive or unnecessarily overcautious.

A trademark is, however, a marketing tool – its prime function is to help sell the product. The marketing team best knows the kind of marks which will satisfy its needs. With the constructive assistance of the legal adviser a powerful marketing weapon can come out of the selection process – a mark that is strong, distinctive and protectable, as well as being appropriate, memorable, easy to pronounce and otherwise effective in marketing terms.

It is advisable, therefore, to take legal advice early in the selection process. Consultation with a trademark adviser will often mitigate, if not avoid, unnecessary expenditures of time and money. To be told just prior to launch that the name for the new product may infringe another's rights, or to be 'hit' with a trademark infringement suit within days or weeks of a project launch can be devastating to the marketing plans for the product, not to mention costly and embarrassing.

The Selection Process

A company will often want to select a brand name that readily suggests the product since such a mark may arguably have greater consumer recall – a very important point, particularly when launching a new product in an otherwise crowded field. A business may also want to develop a new brand name that will fit into an already existing stable of marks. A third consideration may be the image which the company wants to project – futuristic, exciting, wholesome or dependable. One mark may be more attractive than another from this point of view. These, and other business considerations, are often factored into the selection process.

Legal considerations, too, must be part of the equation. The primary legal considerations are:

— the availability of the proposed mark, and
— the relative strength of the mark.

Strong versus Weak Trademarks

There is an established hierarchy of trademarks ranging from strong to weak. Four categories are generally recognised, and are, in descending order:

(1) invented or arbitrary;
(2) suggestive;
(3) descriptive;
(4) generic.

Invented or Arbitrary Marks

An invented or arbitrary trademark is the strongest type of mark. Perhaps the most cited example of an invented mark is Kodak, a word which never existed before. Another, more recent example of an invented mark is Exxon which was specifically created as a replacement for Esso. These marks are 'fanciful' and as such are entitled to broad protection against secondcomers. Other examples are Bic for ballpoint pens, Nike for footwear, Rolex for watches, Samsonite for luggage and Listerine for antiseptic mouthwash.

An 'arbitrary' mark is slightly different in the sense that the word itself may have existed before its use as a trademark but its choice for the product is arbitrary. Zest for soap is a prime example. Other examples are Beefeater for gin, Birds Eye for frozen food, Maestro for motor vehicles, Camel for cigarettes, Apple for computers and Antaeus for male toiletries.

Suggestive Marks

'Suggestive' marks are also considered good marks and are entitled to a wide range of protection. These are favoured by trademark counsel and are often appealing to product managers. For example, Ivory for soap is suggestive of its purity, a central theme in Procter & Gamble's advertising campaigns for the soap. Other examples are Wrangler for jeans, Paper Mate for writing instruments, Visa for credit cards, Lux for soap, Fanta for soft drinks, Flex for shampoo, Eskimo Pie for ice cream and Slalom for razors.

Descriptive Marks

'Descriptive' marks are the most troublesome. As we have noted already product managers often favour descriptive marks because, in a sense, they make their jobs a little easier. They frequently feel that they do not have to work as hard to explain or describe the nature or benefits of the product because the mark already does it for them. Examples of descriptive marks are King Size for men's clothing, Easyload for cameras, Lean 'n' Tender for cooked beef, Comfort for shoes, Kwik-Fit for a tyre fitting service and Hi-Protein for food. Such marks are not generally given protection in law because they describe a physical characteristic or attribute of the product and therefore may not serve the key trademark functions of indicating source of origin of the product.

In the UK and the USA the registration of descriptive marks *per se* is not precluded. Rather the registration of marks which are 'according to their ordinary signification' 'merely' descriptive is precluded. In other words, descriptive trademarks cannot be registered without proof that they have come to distinguish the applicant's products or services. This evidence is known as 'acquired distinctiveness' or 'secondary meaning'. A descriptive mark which has acquired such secondary meaning is registrable. A few examples of such registered marks are Beer Nuts for salted nuts, Nu-Enamel for enamel paint, Little Tavern for restaurant and bar services and Kool for cigarettes.

Generic Marks

The final category is generic marks. There are actually two types of generic marks: those which are generic from their inception and those which have become generic through misuse. 'Soap' is obviously a generic term for a soap product and cannot function as a trademark for those goods. Indeed, some courts have held that the phonetic equivalent of a generic term is also incapable of trademark protection.

It is to avoid genericism that trademark owners are consistently advised by counsel to use the mark as an adjective, not as a noun. Some companies exhort the public likewise. For example, advertisements are often run by the Xerox Corporation advising the public that Xerox is a trademark and should always be used as an adjective: Xerox copier. Similarly, General Foods is careful to advertise some of its products as 'Jell-O brand gelatine' and 'Sanka brand coffee', thus impressing upon the public the brand name status of the marks. In doing so, it is hoped that if these valuable marks are ever challenged as being 'merely generic', courts would find them valid. We discuss in more detail later in this chapter a number of general rules which should be followed by all those responsible for a company's trademarks to ensure that the proprietorship of the mark cannot be undermined.

The other type of generic mark is the mark which, through misuse, has become the common or generic name for the product. The trademark owner, sometimes through his own failure to police his mark or, on other occasions through no fault of his own, may run the risk of losing his mark to genericism. The loss occurs when the public uses the brand name of the product as the name for the product itself. A prime example is 'aspirin' which was once the trademark for a type of pain reliever but, as a result of public misuse, became (in certain countries at least) the name for the product itself. Other terms which are now generic in the USA (though not necessarily elsewhere) but were once valid marks include cellophane, escalator, shredded wheat, and thermos. In a recent and controversial decision, the Ninth Circuit Court of Appeals in the USA has held that Monopoly is a generic term for a real estate board game. (It should be noted, however, that as a result of that decision, the US Trademark Act 1946 (The Lanham Act) has been amended to provide that the primary significance of a registered trademark to the relevant public, rather than purchaser motivation, shall be the test for determining whether that trademark has become the common descriptive name of the relevant goods or services.)

In addition to descriptive marks and generic marks there are other categories of mark which are regarded as legally weak and which should be avoided in the selection process and are noted below.

Laudatory names

Names such as Perfection, Great, Modern, Prestige, Superb, Magnifique, Premium, Silky Soft, Super and Fantastic, should be avoided. They are, generally speaking, incapable of being protected.

Phonetic variations or misspellings of such laudatory words should also be avoided.

Geographical names

These too should be avoided, particularly those which have an association, direct or indirect, with the product, e.g. Detroit for cars, Aspen for ski equipment, Pittsburgh for steel, London for gin or Munich for beer.

Common surnames

If you call your new brand of snackfoods Jones a competitor called Jones may well be able to use the same name. After all, it is his name too! Common surnames should therefore be avoided as you will not, at least until you have established a considerable reputation in a name, be granted exclusive rights to that name to the detriment of others who have claims to it.

Letters and numerals

These are generally considered non-distinctive and are difficult to protect. Trademarks like IBM are rare exceptions and have had the benefit of an extraordinary amount of expenditure over a long, long period. It would be foolhardy to try to emulate their example!

With extensive usage, however, many of the marks categorised above, e.g. surnames, geographical names and letters/numerals have become strong trademarks, e.g. 4711 for eau de cologne, Ford and Cadillac for cars, Hoover for domestic appliances, Philadelphia for cheese, Philips for electrical goods, No. 5 for perfume and Guinness for beer. This usage has been considerable and, in today's competitive environment, it would not generally be sensible to adopt names which, at the outset, are as legally weak as these were in the hope that infringements can be resisted and distinctiveness can thus be acquired.

Misdescriptive, Deceptive or Scandalous Names

Other kinds of names which should be avoided are those which could, even possibly, be regarded as misdescriptive of the product in question or which could give rise to an allegation that use of the mark on the product would lead to deception, e.g. Orlwoola for products which are not all wool, China Therm for non-china products, Realemon for a product not consisting of, in some way, real lemon. Scandalous names which have unpleasant meanings or connotations (even in slang) should also be avoided, e.g. Hallelujah.

TRADEMARK SEARCHING

The availability of a name depends upon whether the identical or a confusingly similar name has already been registered or, in some jurisdictions (notably the USA, UK and other common law based countries) used by another party on the same or similar products. It is therefore necessary, before adopting a name, to conduct thorough searches to determine what marks have already been registered or used in the markets of interest in relation to similar goods and which might give rise to problems.

Your trademark adviser can conduct these searches and any subsequent investigations which may be necessary. If carried out on an international basis such searches can be both expensive and time-consuming. They should not, however, be avoided – to do so would be to jeopardise the whole project.

To determine whether a mark is available in the USA, for example, counsel will conduct a search of the records of the Patent and Trademark Office, trade directories, state trademark registers, 'phone books and other similar sources. A professional search firm with an established library containing such information will almost always be engaged by counsel to conduct the search. The final determination as to whether the mark is available, however, is a legal conclusion which should be made only by experienced trademark counsel.

In reviewing a search report and prior to rendering an opinion on availability, counsel will look at a number of factors:

(1) the nature of the goods or services in question;
(2) their relationship to the goods or services covered by the potentially conflicting mark;
(3) the similarity of the marks in sight, sound or meaning;
(4) the exclusivity of the cited mark;
(5) the inherent strength of the cited mark;
(6) whether a potentially confused mark cited in the search report is, in fact, in use;
(7) any history of prior litigation concerning the proposed mark.

As a rule of thumb, if the goods are identical and the marks are identical or very similar, counsel will in all probability reject the proposed mark. On the other hand, where the goods are unrelated and the marks are distinguishable, counsel will generally approve the mark. Where the goods appear unrelated, but the marks are similar, counsel must determine whether the co-existence of the proposed mark and the prior mark could result in confusion as to the source of origin of the goods. Additionally, counsel must also consider whether the mark itself is weak or strong. A strong mark would be entitled to more deference than a weak one. Distinctive marks like Xerox, Kodak and Exxon, for example, enjoy a much wider 'zone of protection' than suggestive or descriptive marks such as Teltronic, Supa-Sava or Compu-Max.

The fact that a name of interest is already registered by another party does not necessarily mean that the name is unavailable. It simply means that another party at some stage has registered an interest in the name for particular goods or services. The interest may have waned and the registration may no longer be effective, or the company may have gone out of business or into another kind of business. In such cases it may be relatively easy to acquire the earlier trademark and with it the statutory and other rights of the earlier proprietor.

Negotiations with the owner of an already registered conflicting mark, or action to remove that mark from the Register in order to clear the proposed usage, can often take many months to resolve. Important time can therefore be wasted if, at the end of the negotiations, the potential conflict is not resolved. It can also sometimes be costly to clear a name for usage by acquiring the rights established by the owners of existing marks. Generally speaking, if the proposed mark is already registered it may be best simply to abandon it.

ACQUIRING TRADEMARK PROTECTION

Having selected the name for the new product or service and having had appropriate searches and investigations made to ensure that it is available for the proposed usage, the question is then asked: 'How can we protect the name?' There are two methods whereby a trademark can be protected: by registration and by usage.

Registration

By registering a trademark a trademark owner is recording a claim to proprietorship of the mark with the appropriate government authority. In some countries, e.g. France and the Benelux countries, registration is secured merely by depositing an application with the relevant authority. In other countries, notably the UK and the USA, it takes some time to secure registration – after going through an exhaustive examination and opposition process. The resultant registration is, however, a more valuable piece of property than is a simple 'deposit' registration.

It should be borne in mind that in most countries (the USA being an important exception) there is no requirement, at least initially, actually to use the mark in order to secure registration. Unlike other 'use' jurisdictions (e.g. the UK, Canada and Australia) the United States does not recognise 'an intention to use' as the basis for registration of a mark. While limited use of a mark within a small geographical area may be adequate for establishing an exclusive right to use in that geographic area, actual use in interstate commerce is a *sine qua non* to filing an application to register a trademark in the United States Patent and Trademark Office.

In all jurisdictions, however, the cost of filing a trademark is fairly modest – a few hundred dollars – and the benefits can be substantial.

Usage

In certain countries, mainly those whose legal systems are based on English common law principles, it is possible to obtain rights in a trademark through usage – the owner's rights accumulate over time. Trademarks which have not been accepted for registration – for example, on the grounds of their descriptiveness or their surname or geographical significance – may, with extensive usage, come to represent the goodwill of the trademark owner, indicate the product's source of origin and distinguish the goods of one company from those of another. They then acquire a measure of legal 'status'. In the absence of a registration a trademark may be more vulnerable to competitive attack. Moreover, the process of defending such common law rights is a most uncertain one. In practice, the trademark owner should seek even notional registration if at all possible.

WHY REGISTER THE TRADEMARK?

In a large number of countries (e.g. most of Europe, South America, Africa and Japan) if the trademark is not registered the 'owner' of the mark has no rights even if the mark is being used. The only exceptions are in the cases of famous trademarks such as Coca-Cola and Kodak, although even these may be uncertain.

Besides, in countries which follow the British legal system, infringement actions cannot be founded upon unregistered marks even in those countries where such marks can acquire a measure of legal status. Actions must therefore be based on the law of 'unfair competition' or the equivalent law in other jurisdictions, for example 'passing off' in the UK. An unfair competition action is invariably difficult and the outcome is far less easy to predict than an infringement action. This is because, without registration, the rights in a trademark (in those countries where rights can be established by use) arise as a result of the reputation which has been built up in the name.

It is expensive, time-consuming and sometimes simply impossible (in the case, for example, of a new product which has come on to the market without an extensive supporting advertising campaign) to prove such a reputation.

As far as new products in particular are concerned, the rights in a registered trademark ordinarily arise before the mark has been used (a notable exception as indicated above is the USA). If the mark is unregistered and has not been used, obviously no rights can be said to have been established.

In the USA, large corporations, as well as individuals and small firms, which test market many products each year, often take advantage of 'token use'. This is the use of a mark on a small number of goods accompanied by a good faith intention to continue that use within a reasonable period of time.

Under this doctrine, a company can ship a dozen bars of Skana soap to a store in another state on 2 January 1985 and claim that date as a date of first use, even though test marketing of the product may not commence for a few months and nationwide distribution may not begin for a year or more. Since a crucial element is the intention to continue use, no hard or fast rule can be pronounced and each case is weighed on its own merits. The key consideration is whether the 'token use' constituted a *bona fide* sale or shipment at arms length.

A further consideration is that by registering the mark the rest of the world is put on notice that you own it. Accordingly you prevent a third party raising the defence that they innocently adopted the mark. This is called 'constructive notice' in the USA.

Also, the assignment of an unregistered trademark can be uncertain and unsatisfactory in a number of countries. A registered mark, on the other hand, may freely be assigned with or without goodwill in the UK and in most other countries. In the USA, however, it should be noted that an assignment of a mark must include the assignment of the goodwill symbolised by the mark. Assigning a mark without the goodwill is an 'assignment in gross' or a 'naked assignment' which constitutes an abandonment of the mark.

A further benefit of registering a mark is that details concerning registration can in some countries (including the UK and the USA) be deposited with the appropriate Customs authorities. This 'registration' with the Customs in theory means that any goods bearing an apparently infringing mark may be seized and impounded by the Customs authorities upon importation. In an age when trademark infringement and counterfeiting are becoming virtually epidemic, this benefit can be a real one. In practice, however, the United States is the only country where this procedure is so far really effective.

The licensing of a trademark can also be greatly facilitated by registration. A licence often requires a licensor to have registered his mark. Without a registered mark the rights being licensed are necessarily vague.

WHEN SHOULD THE MARK BE REGISTERED?

The registration process should be started as soon as the selected name has been approved by counsel, or, in the USA, as soon as token use has been made. Applications for registration should be filed at that time in all those countries where it is proposed to market the product and where there is a real likelihood that, in the future, the product may be marketed. Registration of a trademark is not a speedy process. In many jurisdictions (including the UK and USA) it takes about eighteen months to two years to complete registration. In other jurisdictions it takes even longer. In Italy, for example, it takes over five years. Even in those countries where registration is a formality and involves simply the deposit of an application (e.g. France and the Benelux countries) it still takes more than six months to secure registration. In most cases, once the registration is secured it is backdated to the date when the original application was filed and the trademark owner's rights in the registered mark run from that date.

It is important therefore to apply for registration without delay in all the markets of interest. Whilst the costs of applying for registration in one country may be modest, if two or three categories or classes of product are to be covered (e.g. it may be prudent in the case of a medicated confectionery product to file applications in both the pharmaceutical and confectionery classes) and a number of countries are involved, in total the costs may be considerable. However, such costs are readily justified when one considers the protection which registration provides. Also, the initial registration offers normally seven to twenty years protection, and the payment of another smaller renewal fee offers protection for extended periods thereafter. Consider too that the costs involved in having to adopt a different trademark in just one or two separate markets could be substantial – not just the time and delay involved in developing a new name but the cost of researching the mark to make sure it is available for use, plus the added cost of creating new packaging and advertising to support the new name. Failure to register the mark in all likely markets also leaves open the possibility of a competitor registering the same or a very similar name in that market and causing serious difficulties as a result.

QUESTIONS OF CLASSIFICATION

It is important for counsel to be informed of the precise nature of the goods or services to be marketed under the name, and into what other fields it is proposed to expand use of the trademark. This information is required to ensure that the product category is correctly and fully described in the application documents and that, eventually, registration for the mark is secured in the right class or classes and for the right goods and/or services.

Most countries nowadays adhere to what is called the International Classification of Goods and Services. If a mark is registered in the wrong class or does not cover a sufficiently broad range of goods within the class concerned, the rights established by registration could well be ineffective in doing what they are supposed to do, i.e. enable the trademark owner's rights to be enforced speedily and avoid a defence being put up by the other side that, for one reason or another, the registration being relied upon is deficient or invalid. It is probably sufficient for our purposes here simply to say that if counsel is given full information on the goods or services in question, problems in this regard should not arise.

IN THE TRADEMARKS OFFICE

The trademark has now been selected and its use has been approved by counsel. Applications have been filed for registration in all the countries of interest. Actual use of the mark can begin. However, the purpose of conducting searches and seeking counsel's advice is to determine whether or not the mark is anticipated by previous registrations and whether it is, therefore, clear to use. Once your counsel gives you the green light you can move ahead with your marketing plans but the actual processes of obtaining registration must be followed.

The procedures before the various national Trademark Offices of the world, other than those which simply operate a 'deposit' system, are very similar. Twelve months or so after the application is filed (and, as mentioned earlier, any registered rights are, in due course, back-dated to the filing date in most countries) it is examined and the applicant is informed whether or not the mark is aceptable for registration; provided the preliminary searches were conducted properly no objections are likely to be raised on the basis of earlier registered marks. If the mark is an inherently strong one (i.e. it is not merely descriptive, geographic or a surname, etc.) it is unlikely to prompt objections. If any such objections are in fact raised they can be argued by counsel.

If the mark is accepted it is then generally published for opposition purposes, though in some countries, e.g. Italy and the Benelux countries, there is no provision for opposition at the Trademark Office and any third parties who object to a registration must raise their objections in court. Provided a mark survives the examination and opposition stages it will become a registered trademark.

PROTECTING AND MAINTAINING THE TRADEMARK

Once the mark is registered, the trademark owner need do little else to preserve his registration other than continue use of his mark. And, as indicated earlier in the chapter, one of the big advantages trademarks have over other forms of intellectual property is their ability to live 'eternally', provided they are properly used and, if registered, renewed from time to time.

If, however, a mark is not used for a number of years, rights to it can be lost. In the USA, for example, non-use for a two year period coupled with the intent not to resume use is deemed evidence of abandonment and is grounds for cancellation of the registration. During the fifth anniversary year of the registration, the owner must file an affidavit of use under Section 8 of the Trademark Act and, if the use has been continuous since registration, the owner may claim the benefit of Section 15 of the Act which renders a registration incontestable – except in some very limited circumstances.

In most other jurisdictions non-usage of a registered mark will mean that the registration becomes effectively unenforceable and vulnerable to cancellation. This period varies from country to country but is usually between two and five years.

Thus whilst registration of a mark is an important first step in the protection process, it is important to use the mark in whatever jurisdictions it is registered, at least from time to time, to ensure that rights in the mark remain effective.

RULES FOR PROPER TRADEMARK USAGE

Bearing in mind the definition of a trademark as being 'a sign or symbol which distinguishes the goods or services of an enterprise', it is important always to make certain that this distinguishing function of the trademark is preserved.

Thus, in addition to use, various procedures should be followed to ensure that rights in the mark are not lost, inadvertently or otherwise. Positive action must be taken by the trademark owner to see that the mark is always used properly by members of his own organisation and by third parties.

In particular, a trademark owner must be sure that his mark does not become the generic name for the product as this would threaten its validity and place it in the public domain, in much the same way as the former trademarks aspirin, kerosene, escalator and cellophane are now in the public domain, at least in many important markets.

It is a relatively simple matter to protect and care for a company's trademarks properly. If followed consistently the following rules should protect a company from the loss of any of its trademark rights.

Rule 1   A trademark must, wherever and whenever it appears in print, be distinguished from its surrounding text.

   This rule applies not only to advertising copy, on-pack instructions, brochures, etc. but also to internal memoranda and general correspondence. Thus the trademark must always be capitalised (or at least have its first letter capitalised), italicised, be given bold-face print or be placed in quotation marks.

   Probably the easiest approach is simply to capitalise the mark on all occasions it appears in print. The generic name of the product should not be capitalised and nor should its first letter(s), e.g.:

   Proper use   With effective marketing techniques Apple computers have sold extremely well.

   Improper use   With effective marketing techniques apple computers have sold extremely well.

Rule 2   Always follow the trademark with the common generic (i.e. the dictionary) name of the product, e.g.:

Proper use	Vaseline petroleum jelly has many uses.
Improper use	Vaseline has many uses.

Rule 3 Trademarks should always be used as adjectives, never as nouns, e.g.:

Proper use	Get into Wrangler jeans now!
Improper use	Get into Wranglers now!

Rule 4 A trademark should never be used as a verb, e.g.:

Proper use	Copies from the Xerox copier are excellent.
Improper use	The Xeroxed copies are excellent.

Rule 5 A trademark should never be used in the plural, e.g.:

Proper use	Take two Anadin analgesics and go to bed.
Improper use	Take two Anadins and go to bed.

Rule 6 A trademark should never be used in the possessive, e.g.:

Proper use	Compaq computer's extraordinary features . . .
Improper use	Compaq's extraordinary features . . .

Rule 7 The graphic design of a trademark should always be strictly adhered to. Do not use a proliferation of different graphic treatments for the same trademark.

Rule 8 So as to avoid any doubt as to ownership of a trademark, give notice to the world that the word or symbol being used as a trademark is, in fact, a trademark
— where the trademark is registered the ® symbol or an asterisk should be used.
— where the trademark is not registered (or is awaiting registration) but you regard it as your exclusive property, the ™ symbol should be used in place of the ® symbol.
In addition to the use of these symbols more formal notice should be given in printed matter by spelling out the proprietary status of the mark in a footnote, e.g.:

Cariba ®

® Cariba is a registered trademark of Schweppes Ltd

Rule 9 The spelling of a trademark should never be changed, a new word should not be formed from it and its form should never be modified, e.g.:

The Xerox trademark should not, as a result of a copywriter's whim, suddenly acquire an additional letter and become Xeroxx nor should it be hyphenated to Xer-ox. Similarly, in usage, a trademark such as Mercedes-Benz should not be abbreviated to Merc.

RECORD KEEPING

In addition to ensuring that the trademark is being used properly in broad accordance with the rules mentioned above, it is advisable that records are kept to determine at any given time the total sales of products bearing the trademark. It is recommended that, as a general rule, the trademark appears on all invoices and that an ongoing record (as suggested above) is kept of all invoices. The purpose of keeping such records is to be able to prove, if necessary, that the mark has been used on a continuing basis for however many years and in whatever countries. Written records of this kind can be invaluable to trademark counsel in the prosecution of trademarks through to registration, in opposition proceedings and in litigation.

Furthermore, it is good practice to keep copies of all advertisements, promotional items, product literature, packaging materials, price lists, badges, etc. relating to the product bearing the trademark. This information, if readily available and identifiable, can be of considerable assistance in the maintenance of international trademark rights.

POLICING THE TRADEMARK

As well as using his trademark correctly, a trademark owner should take care to ensure that his rights in the mark are not infringed by third parties. This can severely narrow, if not eliminate, the scope of protection to which the mark is entitled, or even worse, render the mark abandoned. Returning to our Zest soap example, the trademark owner should be careful that others do not use the identical mark Zest on shampoo, a seemingly related product; or use the similar name Zist on soap – each of which could weaken the Zest mark.

A trademark is a valuable asset and can lead to expanded business opportunities. The Ivory soap mark, for instance, has expanded to Ivory liquid detergent for dishes and Ivory Snow Flakes detergent for clothes. It is important, therefore, that potential avenues of expansion are not blocked.

The sales force is the frontline of a company and acts very much as its eyes. It must be alert to misuses and abuses of the company's trademarks – whether by competitors or by those dealing with the company, e.g. licensees, retailers, suppliers and distributors. Any instances of misuse and abuse should be drawn immediately to the attention of the company's trademark advisers.

LITIGATION

Litigation in all jurisdictions is expensive. It is more expensive in some countries (e.g. the USA) than in others but what is certain is that if, to preserve your trademark rights, you need to start an infringement suit (or if you are taken to court by another party seeking to protect its own trademark rights), it will cost a lot of money and management time.

Sometimes, however, it cannot be avoided. Where a company's trademark is at stake and the business associated with it is in danger of being eroded, or where the trademark owner's reputation is being jeopardised, prompt action through the courts is essential. It is in these cases that a company's trademark position must be strongly asserted.

There is a misconception among many people, including some involved in trademark management, that because a trademark is registered it is somehow sacrosanct – that the act of registration is all that is required and, once effected, no further action is necessary. This is not the case at all. Registration of a trademark, as mentioned above, confers upon the proprietor an exclusive right to use the mark in respect of the goods or services for which it is registered. If, however, a third party uses the identical or similar mark to the registered mark there is no miraculous judicial order issued from a higher authority which automatically stops that third party usage. Rather, the burden of enforcing trademark rights is always on the original owner whether or not the trademark is registered.

In the main, there are two kinds of action which can be started in jurisdictions throughout the world to protect trademark rights – those based on a registration, and those based on common law rights. The first of these are generally referred to as 'infringement' actions, the others as 'unfair competition' (or in some jurisdictions, notably the UK, as 'passing off') actions.

Infringement

To sue for infringement of statutory trademark rights it is necessary to have a trademark registered for the goods or services in relation to which the alleged infringing use is being made. In the UK and jurisdictions which have a UK based law, statutory trademark rights are limited to the precise goods or services which are covered by the registration; for example, if the Cariba mark is registered for 'non-alcoholic drinks' in the UK the owner of that mark cannot sue a third party for infringement if that third party uses the Cariba mark on a can of beer or a bottle of wine. Its rights would be limited to the common law action of 'passing off'.

This underlines the need to ensure that the coverage of the registration (i.e. the statutory rights in the mark) is as broad in scope as possible. The only real limitation to the scope of protection obtained is that, in most jurisdictions, it is necessary to show or at least claim some *bona fide* intention to use the mark on the goods or services listed in the specification.

In infringement proceedings in the USA and other countries, the test as to whether a third party's use of the mark in question is infringement is generally whether that usage is likely to lead to confusion, mistake or deception. Thus, if a mark is registered in the USA for 'a shampoo' and a third party uses a very similar mark on a hand cream, an eye shadow or a deodorant, such usage would still be held to constitute infringement if the registrant can prove that there is actual confusion or a likelihood of confusion arising in the market-place.

Unfair Competition or 'Passing Off'

These actions are usually begun in the following circumstances:

(1) where the plaintiff's mark is not registered;
(2) where it is registered but does not cover the defendant's goods;
(3) where the defendant's trade dress (i.e. get-up) is very similar to that used by the plaintiff (the trademarks themselves may or may not be similar);
(4) where the defendant's actions generally are calculated to benefit unfairly from the plaintiff's goodwill and reputation.

In such actions, the trademark owner must prove, in essence, three things:

(1) that he has established a reputation (or goodwill) in the trademark or trade dress in question;
(2) that the use by the defendant of the similar mark or 'get-up' has caused, or is likely to cause, confusion in the market-place;
(3) that the trademark owner has suffered, or is likely to suffer, damage as a result of the defendant's activity.

If the trademark owner can prove these three things, he will ordinarily be granted the relief sought.

It is worth mentioning, however, that there are some conceptual differences between the law of 'passing off' as it applies in the UK and similar jurisdictions and the law of 'unfair competition' as it exists in the United States and elsewhere. Generally speaking (and perhaps not surprisingly!), the latter recognises the concept of 'unfairness' more than does the former; the UK courts appear more concerned with the result of the actions complained of in terms of direct financial damage rather than with the intent of or the benefit to the defendant. For example, the owner of a 'marque notoire' (a continental European concept), such as Rolls-Royce or Hoover, would very likely be able to enjoin the use in the United States or a continental European country of those marks on goods with which he does not and would not be perceived to have any connection, simply on the basis that the defendant's actions are clearly calculated to benefit unfairly from the trademark owner's goodwill and reputation and that such goodwill and reputation might in the long term be damaged in some unquantifiable way. In the UK, the outcome of any such action based on the law of 'passing off' might very well be different.

REMEDIES

In most cases the purpose of going to court is to stop the defendant continuing his objectionable commercial activity. What the trademark owner is seeking, therefore, is an injunction, an order restraining the defendant from using the mark in question. If his case is strong enough he will be granted such an injunction in most jurisdictions.

The trademark owner may also be granted an order for the delivery up for destruction of, or for the erasure or obliteration of the mark on, any infringing goods in the possession of or under the control of the defendant, as well as of any deceptive labels, advertising materials, etc.

Finally, the trademark owner may obtain an order for an inquiry as to damages in respect of the past interference with his rights by the defendant, or for an account of the profits made by the defendant from the sale of the infringing goods.

Under most judicial systems there is provision to apply for an injunction to be granted which will temporarily restrain a defendant's commercial activity until such time as a full hearing of the action can be undertaken. This interim hearing is then followed up by a full trial of the action to determine the merits of the case and whether a final injunction will be granted. Often, but certainly not always, the interim hearing will end the dispute. If the trademark owner works quickly and obtains impressive evidence that his business will be irreparably damaged if the defendant is allowed to pursue his activity, the court will often grant an interim injunction. Under such circumstances the infringer, having been restrained, will simply abandon the project, or settle in a manner satisfactory to the trademark owner.

It should be borne in mind that in the UK and a number of other countries, the courts at the interim stage are not solely concerned with the legal merits of a case but also with what is loosely referred to as the 'balance of convenience'. In other words, while there must be a reasonable chance of success at the full hearing, the economic consequences to the parties of the granting or refusal of an interim injunction and their respective abilities financially to compensate each other in costs and damages are major considerations.

CONCLUSIONS

In the broad area of marketing, nowhere else do the marketing man and the lawyer come closer together than in the area of branding. And nowhere else does the law afford those involved in marketing such powerful rights in the defence of valuable assets. Curiously, however, the relationship between marketing people, on the one hand, and trademark lawyers, on the other, is frequently tenuous or even hostile. It would pay each side to understand and communicate with the other, for by doing so both they and their companies stand to gain the considerable advantages afforded under trademark law.

5 Making Your Brands Work Harder

LAURENCE HEFTER

TRADEMARK LICENSING, FRANCHISING AND COLLATERAL EXPLOITATION

Both franchising and collateral exploitation of trademarks are forms of the broad practice of trademark and service mark licensing. (For the sake of simplicity, trademarks and service marks will be discussed under the broad term trademarks.) Trademark licensing, in general, is the practice of permitting others to use one's trademarks on approved goods under terms which enable the trademark owner to control the quality of the licensed goods.

The enormous industry of franchising centres around the licensing of trademarks to several licensees in different geographical areas. Along with the right to use the trademarks goes the obligation to use the marks only in a certain way and style. Usually, the franchise agreement also grants to the licensee ('franchisee') the right to use the business system developed by the licensor ('franchisor'). Depending upon the nature of the franchised business, the franchise agreement may require the franchisee to use the franchisor's trade dress, exterior building design, interior decor, employee uniforms or to provide products which meet certain standards set by the franchisor. The franchisee often is given the right to use the franchisor's proprietary information, such as instruction manuals or recipes, and other materials related to the running of the franchise, such as business and tax advice and shared advertising. The McDonalds fast food restaurants are an excellent example of a franchise.

Collateral exploitation of trademarks, on the other hand, is the practice of licensing primarily well-known trademarks for use on goods unrelated to the goods in connection with which the marks have achieved their fame. Many owners of popular trademarks have elected to broaden the line of products on which their marks are used, thereby enhancing the strength of their marks and enjoying additional financial and advertising benefits. Such collateral exploitation of their marks has been achieved by contracting with others to permit use of their popular trademarks on a wide variety of products. Use of the well-known Coca-Cola or Budweiser logos, which achieved their fame on beverages, on T-shirts, hats, mirrors and tote bags, to name only a few products, are examples of collateral exploitation of trademarks through licensing.

Another form of trademark licensing is merchandising and character licensing, such as licensing the use of the popular E.T. movie character or the comic strip character Superman on lunch boxes, key rings, dolls, bicycles, video games, etc. Indeed, some characters have been developed for the sole purpose of licensing their use on various types of merchandise. For example, the Strawberry Shortcake character had no life before it was used under licence on greeting cards, dolls, lunch boxes and many other items.

THE IMPORTANCE OF REGISTERING THE LICENSED MARK

Obviously, one must own trademark rights in order to be able to license them and, therefore, the licensor must be certain that he has the right to license the mark before entering into a licence agreement. As discussed in an earlier chapter, in most countries rights to a mark are determined by registration. In some countries, including the United States, the first user of the mark is the owner of that mark for the goods on which the mark was used and in the geographical area where the mark was used. Therefore, the prospective licensor should first conduct an in-depth search to be sure no one has prior rights in the mark for use on the goods which will be the subject of a licence. He should then apply for, if he hasn't already obtained, a registration for the mark to cover those specific goods.

In the United States, once the mark is used in interstate commerce, a federal registration can be obtained which will convey nationwide ownership except for previous users of that mark. However, if an applicant applies for a registration in a country foreign to the USA where he is a citizen or has a place of business, he can then apply for registrations in other countries, including the United States, based upon that application. This permits him to obtain a registration in the United States even though the mark has never been used. This is the one exception to US law which normally requires use of a trademark before a registration can be obtained and before any rights can be claimed in that mark.

If a company is considering licensing its marks for use on collateral goods, it is particularly important for that company to obtain registration for the collateral goods. Most countries do not recognise licensing the use of trademarks for goods which are not covered by a registration or on which the licensor has not previously used the mark. In the United States, although a recent spate of cases recognise the licensing of well-known marks for use on collateral goods, it still is a preferred practice for the trademark owner to be the first to use the mark on each type of collateral goods in order to establish trademark rights and to obtain a registration for those goods.

LICENSING FUNDAMENTALS

Since a trademark indicates the source of origin of the goods, it may be curious how one can license a trademark for use by others and have the trademark maintain its principal function, namely indication of source. By requiring the trademark owner to control the nature and quality of the goods or services with which the mark is used, the concept of identification of source is maintained. That is why the trademark owner must have the legal right as well as ability to control the nature and quality of the licensed goods or services.

The following types of clauses are recommended for all types of trademark licensing agreements:

(1) Preamble

This clause should state why the agreement is in being and why the parties are interested in a licensing arrangement. The interests of the trademark licensor, the reasons why the licence agreement is being entered into and why others are being allowed to use the mark should be identified.

(2) Identification of the Licensed Mark, Goods and Services

The trademark and the nature of the goods or services which are being licensed should be clearly identified. If possible, registration or application numbers should be used for identification and illustrations of the trademarks or copies of the registrations should be attached to the agreement. The agreement should also be very specific as to limitations placed upon the type of goods or services in connection with which the licensor permits the licensee to use the mark.

(3) Licence Grant

Since the licensor may grant an exclusive, sole or non-exclusive licence, the agreement should indicate specifically which type of licence is being granted. Under a non-exclusive licence, the licensee is granted the right to use the mark; however, others can be granted the same rights. Under an exclusive licence, the licensee is given the exclusive right to use the mark, exclusive even as to the licensor unless expressly provided otherwise. Under a sole licence, the licence grant runs only to the licensee and to no one else but it does not preclude the licensor from using the mark. Rather than relying upon the understood definitions of these terms, it is recommended, particularly when the rights of the licensor to use his own mark are at stake, that the terms be specifically defined in the agreement. Also, since it is virtually impossible and economically prohibitive in the United States to determine if someone has previously used a mark, the licensor should disclaim warranties with respect to the rights of third parties or, instead of granting an exclusive licence, agree only not to grant other licences.

(4) Territorial Limitations

Unless a licensing agreement specifically contains a clause limiting the licensed territory, it will be presumed that a trademark registration – which is effective nationwide – is being licensed throughout the country of registration. In the USA, attempts to place territorial restrictions upon use of a licensed trademark can pose anti-trust risks which, in many cases, can be overcome if care is paid to this issue.

(5) Quality Control

It is fundamental that a trademark licence contain quality control provisions. However, not only must the provision be written into the agreement, it must be enforced.

Obviously, such control also protects the reputation of the licensor and the trademark. It may also help to protect the licensor from liability resulting from damage caused by a product by ensuring proper manufacturing and construction of all licensed goods. However, too much control usually is not welcomed by the licensee and over-control of a licensee might also present anti-trust problems in the USA.

Product liability of licensors is an area of law which is growing rapidly, and licensors are increasingly being held accountable in product liability actions for injuries and other damages caused by products manufactured by licensees. The greater the controls exercised by the licensor, the greater the likelihood that the licensor will be held liable. If the controls imposed upon the licensee exceed the needs for control of the quality of licensed products or services, a good argument can be made that, to the public, the licensee may appear to be nothing more than an agent of the licensor and, therefore, the licensor should be held accountable for damages arising out of use of these products or services.

Licensor liability can be a particular problem in the area of collateral product licensing. To begin with, the licensor is often not sufficiently knowledgeable about the licensed products to be able to provide adequate quality control since collateral products do not fall within the normal business and expertise of the licensor. Furthermore, in the United States many courts are inclined to hold the trademark owner liable under a product liability theory where it is shown that the owner/licensor benefits from the licensee's use of the mark.

To minimise risk of liability, potential collateral product licensees and their products should be screened carefully. The licensor may even wish to retain an independent testing laboratory or consultant to assist in product approval. Also, some trademark owners have not required royalty payments for use of their marks on collateral products so they can argue as a defence to a product liability claim that they have not received any economic benefits from the licence. Instead, the licensor views the licence as a means to obtain free advertising and to broaden the scope of protection for the mark.

With regard to controlling the quality of products, the licensor should provide the licensee with standards and the licence agreement should specify that failure to maintain these standards is a breach of the agreement. The licensor should also provide for frequent, random sampling of products so that he can be apprised of the true quality of the products. While not part of the agreement, it is a good practice for the licensor to make random purchases of licensed products or services on the open market to keep apprised of the quality being offered the public. The licensor also should have the right to make random, unannounced inspections of the licensee's plant to see what really goes on behind those closed doors. If a product requires the use of a key ingredient which is not suitable to being defined in specifications, such as a secret formula or a unique taste, the product quality can be controlled in part by requiring that the ingredient be purchased from approved or specified sources of supply or, in certain instances, from the licensor himself.

It is more difficult to control the quality of services than products. Service mark licensees should be trained on the subject of how the licensor expects the licensed services to be performed. It is particularly important that a licensor be careful to exercise sufficient control to ensure quality service, but to avoid the outward appearance to the public of the existence of an agency relationship. Quality controls, if properly handled, can also be used to control the specific products being sold under a service mark.

(6) Indemnification

Because there is a substantial likelihood a licensor will be found liable for damages caused by a licensed product, it is advisable that a licensor obtain indemnification from licensees for production liability or tort liability. The indemnification should extend beyond the term of the agreement, or at least should cover damages or injuries which occurred, or which resulted from products made, during the agreement term. The licensor also should require the licensee to carry product liability insurance, to name the licensor as co-insured in the licensee's insurance policy and to require the insurance company to notify the licensor in the event that premiums are not paid or the policy is being terminated. This will then allow the licensor to pay the premiums or somehow otherwise insure himself to avoid losing the benefits of insurance.

(7) Trademark Usage

It is very important that a licensor control and actively police the style of the use of the mark, that is, the colour, typeface, dimensions, proportions and positioning of the mark so that the public is exposed to a uniform usage. Regarding the latter consideration, it is important that the licensed mark be positioned so as not to be confused or associated with the licensee's own trademark, if any, which is affixed to the same goods as is the licensed mark.

The licensor should also require the licensee to indicate the nature or status of a particularly trademark (e.g. whether the mark is registered and by whom it is owned). This is especially important in the area of collateral product licensing, where a mark is often registered only for certain goods but not those covered by the licence. The registered trademark symbol ® should not be used on goods for which the mark is not registered. For example, if the mark is registered only for use on soft drinks, the ® symbol should not be used when the mark is used on clothing or toys. In such situations, an application to register the mark for use on the new goods should be filed promptly and another notice, such as the letters TM, should be used with the mark until a registration is issued.

The licensor should also ensure that the licensee complies with rules of proper trademark usage in order to avoid jeopardising the mark by virtue of such improper usage (as discussed earlier, the mark should not be used as an adjective or in a plural form and should always be accompanied by a generic term for the goods with which the mark is used, etc.).

To ensure proper use of the mark, the licensor's prior approval of advertising and other printed material should be obtained before the marks are used.

The licensor should also require that a notice be used identifying it as the owner of the mark. This can be done by using an asterisk and an identifying phrase such as 'Mark is the trademark of XYZ Company' or 'Mark owned by and used under licence from XYZ Company'.

The licensor should also forbid the use of the mark as part of the licensee's trade name because it is very difficult, upon termination of an agreement, to get a licensee to terminate the use of his trade name. Such use also tends to diffuse the significance of the mark.

(8) Acknowledgement of Title

The licensee should agree that all uses of the mark flow to the benefit of the licensor and that the licensor owns the mark. The licensee should also agree to take no actions which will be adverse to the licensor's interest or ownership in the mark.

(9) Termination

Many agreements provide for termination of the agreement for non-compliance and give a period of time after notice of non-compliance in which to cure the default. However, it may not always be a good idea to provide such a period. There are certain actions which ought to trigger immediate termination of the licence, without affording a cure period. The theory is that some kinds of defaults are, by nature, incurable: deliberate false statements or misrepresentations, misuse of marks, abandonment of the business and bankruptcy (although clauses automatically terminating the agreement upon bankruptcy may be unenforceable in the USA). The licensor preferably should reserve the right to terminate for any reason and without cause by giving a predetermined notice.

Upon termination, the rights of the licensor and the licensee should be clear. There should be an immediate cessation of all use of the mark by the licensee, and the licensee should be required to return to the licensor everything bearing the mark. Such a provision is less objectional to licensees if the licensor helps to pay for goods or printed matter that must be returned. The licensee may be permitted to sell his goods over a limited period of time after if they are approved products and of the proper quality.

The licence agreement should also specify that the licensor is entitled to temporary or permanent injunctions, as well as other relief, if the licensee fails to cease using the mark when obligated to do so.

Finally, a licensor will often wish, particularly in franchise situations, to require the licensee to forfeit a valuable location, or to transfer its telephone number and listings to the licensor. These situations should, if possible, be anticipated in the agreement.

LINE EXTENSION

While not a form of licensing, line extension is another approach frequently used to benefit from the reputation of well-known marks. Line extension is the practice by which a trademark owner extends the use of its mark to new products. For instance, the Coca-Cola Company recently extended use of its famous Coke mark to its new diet colas and caffeine-free colas. Although line extension can provide instant product recognition and customer acceptance of new products, such new uses of established trademarks should be made only after very careful consideration. The Coca-Cola Company, for instance, chose another mark, Tab, for its diet colas and avoided the use of its Coke and Coca-Cola marks on this product for many years. Only recently has the Coca-Cola Company extended use of the Coke mark to other cola products in its line, namely diet drinks.

When contemplating a possible line extension, the trademark owner should consider, first, whether extension of the mark to other products will dilute the strength of the mark, secondly, whether problems with the new products could damage the reputation of the mark once it is applied to the goods (e.g. use of an established mark on a product later found to be defective, dangerous or a failure could damage the reputation of the original product and the substantial goodwill built up in the mark over many years), and thirdly, whether use of the mark on the new goods is fundamentally inconsistent with use of the mark on the original goods (e.g. use of a mark originally used for aspirin-free pain relievers on a new pain reliever product containing aspirin).

In the proper situation, use of a well-known mark on a line extension product can bring instant commercial success to that new product.

FINAL THOUGHTS

In the mid-1980s retail sales of licensed goods in the USA were $40 billion, up from $6.5 billion in 1979. The growth of licensing is on a similar scale around the world. In Japan, the usage of licensed trademarks is staggering; in Britain, names like Harrods and Slazenger are being used, under licence, more widely than their owners would have considered possible only a few years before. Clearly the opportunities for brand owners for licensing and collateral exploitation are enormous, but in legal terms the pitfalls are many. Handled properly, however, the rewards can be considerable.

6 Commercial Counterfeiting

VINCENT CARRATU

INTRODUCTION

> The nefarious but lucrative business of pirating or counterfeiting genuine trademark goods has too long flourished unchecked to the incalculable injury of every consumer, of every honest merchant, manufacturer, and trader, and has extensively multiplied costly and tedious litigation.

This statement is part of a petition which was presented to the United States Congress in 1876. It was signed by the principal manufacturers of New York, Boston and Philadelphia in their attempt to force the enactment of criminal sanctions against product counterfeiters. It could just as easily be included in a petition submitted today. Its message is as important and the problem even worse. The United States was not the only country to recognise this problem. In the United Kingdom, a draft Trade Mark Bill was drawn up in 1862 and actually became law in 1875. In France, the Union des Fabricants was established during the same period specifically to protect French industry against the counterfeiting of its products; the Union is still active today.

There is a great deal of confusion as to what is actually meant by product or commercial counterfeiting. Basically, it is where copies, usually inferior, are represented as being merchandise of the original producer with the deliberate intent to deceive consumers and 'steal' business from the producer. A similar offence, known as 'passing off', is where products presented in a confusingly similar fashion are sold to consumers who are misled into thinking that these products are the genuine article. In civil law countries passing off is known as 'unfair competition'. For our purposes, counterfeit goods fall within both of the above definitions.

Commercial counterfeiting is always an infringement of a manufacturer's trademark but may also include an infringement of his copyright, patent or design. In some pharmaceutical cases, every one of the above rights may be infringed.

HISTORICAL BACKGROUND

From time immemorial producers of objects of value have identified and protected their works by the use of distinctive names, words, or designs. They have thus branded their products. The word 'brand' derives from the Anglo-Saxon 'to burn', and it was by this method that early man marked this livestock. From the branding of his livestock he moved on to brand his works. Museums have numerous examples of articles bearing their producer's marks. These range from Egyptian, Greek and Roman gold and silver jewellery, to pottery, lead pipes, bricks and even foods, and it is possible that the ealiest known use of marks were those found on some Transylvanian pottery jars, made more than 7000 years ago. It was, however, during the Roman era that the true value of affixing one's mark on products was first recognised.

Once consumers realised that one brand of product was better or worse than another, they started asking for articles by name; brand selling was born. Producers of inferior goods soon realised that they were at a disadvantage and they quickly saw the benefit of affixing another person's mark to their own inferior products. Museums throughout the world have examples of early counterfeits. One can see imitation Roman pottery produced in Belgium in the early part of the first century BC, before the Roman Conquest of Britain, which was then exported to Britain. The imitators failed to appreciate the significance of the signs they used; they merely jumbled letters but they obviously deceived the Britons to whom they were sold. Belgium is still the home of counterfeit pottery – the majority of spurious Capo di Monte figurines seen today originated in that country! From these small beginnings, an entire industry has developed. An industry which, in recent years, has enjoyed phenomenal growth.

Commercial counterfeiters are frequently referred to as 'pirates' and piracy is the generic term used to describe their activities, particularly within the entertainment industry where video and audio copying is almost endemic. Today's pirates are as devious and dangerous as those of bygone days. They resort to any number of subterfuges to confuse those trying to catch them, even to the extent of setting up false front companies to monitor the activities of their pursuers. They will if necessary even resort to violence. In the Far East and Latin America it is quite usual for the manufacture and shipment of counterfeit goods to be protected by armed guards. Even in Europe counterfeiters have been found to be armed.

It is this development which is the most alarming. The general view used to be that counterfeiters were mainly proprietors of businesses in urgent need of new markets who succumbed to temptation. That may have been the case years ago but not now. The present day pirate is usually a person who has deliberately set out to copy another's products, whatever they may be. Today he will produce false Chanel perfumes, tomorrow he will switch to counterfeit Fila sports shirts, then later he will import fake Dunlop tennis rackets from

Pakistan. Variety is his spice of life and the rewards phenomenal. Hence the interest shown in these offences by organised crime.

Evidence of counterfeiting can be seen throughout the world. Inferior sports shirts bearing the Lacoste, Adidas or Fila logos are widely available. They may look the part but after their first wash the value of buying the genuine article is soon appreciated. There are fake Levi jeans which come apart within weeks; counterfeit Slazenger tennis rackets that collapse during the first match; imitation Ferodo brake linings that need to be replaced within a few hundred miles; and fake Louis Vuitton luggage that falls apart during the first trip. Some counterfeit articles, however, are as good as the original, if not better. During a recent case in Spain counterfeit leathergoods were seized bearing an internationally famous brand name – Gucci. They were so good that even the genuine producers were confused. In Italy we were shown a counterfeit Rolex watch which has been keeping excellent time for more than twenty years without having been serviced once.

GENUINE COUNTERFEITS

It is not unknown for counterfeiters to obtain genuine reject products which they then alter so that they can be sold as first quality merchandise. A recent case involved Royal Doulton porcelain. Royal Doulton only sell their seconds to staff but before doing so they remove their trade-marks. The counterfeiters skilfully reinstated the marks using epoxy resin fillers and enamel. The new marks were virtually undetectable on first inspection and many expert dealers were deceived. Second quality figurines selling for less than £10.00 each became approved products fetching over £70.00 each.

THE OVERRUN

Another problem is that of 'overruns'. Many companies use outside contractors to produce their goods; this is particularly so in the clothing industry. Fashion houses have their silk scarves and ties produced in Italy; jeans are manufactured in Asia and South America; the leather industry has its handbags and luggage made in Italy, Spain or Morocco. The total production of these articles is the property of the trademark owner, but the extra few thousand pieces produced at the end of the day, or even overnight – the 'overruns' – are often considered by local management and staff as being a legitimate 'bonus'.

Although they are produced by the appointed manufacturers they are still false as the use of the trademark on these items was not authorised by the trademark owner. Identifying such products from the genuine ones in an impossible task.

ECONOMIC DAMAGE CAUSED BY COMMERCIAL
COUNTERFEITING

The January 1984 Report of the US International Trade Commission put the
losses suffered by US companies as a result of product counterfeiting at
between $6–8 billion each year. The situation within Europe is equally
serious. Between November 1982 and June 1984, the UK's Trading Standards
Service was responsible for 13 948 convictions involving product counterfeiting. The resulting fines and costs totalled £621 671, while more than £2 000 000
worth of counterfeit goods were seized or surrendered. Over half of that total
was made up of counterfeit video and audio tapes. Yet the Trading Standards
Service only dealt with a fraction of the problem.

LEGAL SITUATION

Almost every country in the world now has some form of trademark
legislation but not all this legislation is effective. Latin America, where
product counterfeiting is endemic, is bound by the Inter-American Convention of 1929 which was based on French law. The signatories only grant
protection to those trademark owners who can prove use of their marks in
certain Latin American countries within a specified period after registration,
and continual use thereafter. These provisions are familiar to infringers who
have put them to wide use. In Mexico, for example, bogus Cartier stores and
fake Gucci and Lacoste boutiques abounded both in Mexico City and
throughout the country. In some Far Eastern countries the laws are just as
weak. The Taiwanese Government for example has taken steps to combat
counterfeiting but these have been neither sufficiently aggressive nor effectively pursued.

CURRENT SITUATION

The last thirty years have seen an explosion in commercial counterfeiting. We
have witnessed improved sophistication and organisation on the part of the
counterfeiters, a wider international scope and a massive increase in their size
and diversity. They are no longer cottage industries but multinational
businesses which, in organisation and know-how, can compete on equal terms
with many of today's major corporations.

Designer Sportswear Inc, a New York based counterfeiter of jeans, had
more than 500 retailers distributing its merchandise. The proprietor and his
associates supervised the entire operation, including the bribing of bankers
and the obtaining of false credit references. In a recent international perfume
case counterfeiters were financed by 'black' money to set up operations in

Italy, Spain, Mexico and the United Kingdom. Their raw materials came from various countries and their distribution networks were located in Luxembourg and the Middle East. The entire business was controlled in a highly professional manner; the quality of their merchandise was exceptional.

There are many reasons for this rapid growth in commercial counterfeiting. New offset printing machinery, for example, has enabled counterfeiters to print duplicate product labels very similar to the originals. New manufacturing techniques have allowed the low-cost production of products where formerly massive investment in plant was required. Moreover, product counterfeiting has become an important part of the economies of a number of countries, particularly those in South East Asia, Latin America and also in parts of Europe. Recently in northern Italy a well-known company was prosecuted for counterfeiting branded silks. The case, however, was dismissed because 'the company employs more than three hundred people and, as such, is an important part of the community and its economy'. It must also be remembered that counterfeiting provides an attractive source of hard currency. This is of extreme interest to all third-world countries as well as to the Eastern bloc.

THE COUNTERFEITER'S PRODUCTS

Counterfeiting has now spread from luxury branded goods to a wide range of industrial and commercial items and has even been directly responsible for a number of deaths. The American Medical Association has evidence of at least twelve deaths due to counterfeit drugs and in the developing world there may have been thousands more. Also, fourteen aeroplane crashes and at least two deaths have been traced to counterfeit aviation parts, hundreds of heart pumps have been recalled due to dangerous fake components and the coffee crop of Kenya was ruined in 1978 when it was treated with useless counterfeit fungicide. Dunlop, Hoffman La Roche, ICI, Adidas, Kodak, Chanel, Bell Helicopters, Rolex, Dior, Louis Vuitton, Gucci and Levi Strauss are just a few of the victim companies.

PERFUMES

The counterfeiter does not waste time copying a little known product. He chooses one that is a household name on which the trademark owner has spent millions in promotion. He also selects products that are easy to copy, cheap to produce, simple to distribute, but of high value. Perfumes meet all these criteria. Every perfume house has display cabinets filled with counterfeits. Within the last few years there have been successful prosecutions against counterfeiters of Chanel, Estée Lauder, Elizabeth Arden, Helena Rubinstein, Dior, Jean Patou and many other fragrance products.

DRINKS

Spirits, liqueurs, champagnes and wines are also favoured by the counter-feiter. It was during prohibition in the United States that organised crime made its first sortie into liquor counterfeiting. The Federal Authorities seized the contraband drinks smuggled into the country from Canada, Europe and elsewhere so the syndicates had to look elsewhere for their supplies. Illicit stills proliferated but their 'moonshine' was not acceptable to sophisticated society. It was a logical step for the organisers to present their 'moonshine', suitably flavoured and in containers and packaging which would confuse but satisfy their discerning customers. Counterfeit Johnnie Walker, Cutty Sark, and other well-known brands became popular in the 'speakeasies'.

When the National Prohibition Act (the Volstead Act), was finally repealed in December 1933 the need to counterfeit drinks vanished but counterfeiters had tasted the rewards. Counterfeit branded drinks can still be found in many countries. The Italian police, for example, recently seized large quantities of counterfeit Johnnie Walker whisky, both Red and Black Label, which had been produced at a state-owned distillery near Sophia, Bulgaria and then shipped to the free port of Trieste for onward transmission to Africa.

PHARMACEUTICALS

Pharmaceutical companies spend billions of dollars developing new drugs for human and animal use. Selling prices must reflect these enormous costs and can therefore be extremely high when compared with actual production costs. This is appreciated by those unscrupulous individuals who are prepared to abuse the owner's patent and trademark rights.

The enforcement of patent rights can be complicated, time consuming and expensive. Patents on average have a twenty-year life-span and can either be concerned with the product in its entirety (i.e. product patents) or with the process used to manufacture the active ingredient (i.e. process patents). In most developed countries both forms of patent are available but there are exceptions, notably Austria, Finland, Greece, Norway, Portugal and Spain, plus the Eastern bloc countries and most of the Middle East, Latin America and Asia. None of these countries has product patents while at least twenty-eight countries in the world have no patent laws whatsoever.

Manufacturers in these countries produce and sell a pure active compound as a 'generic product'. It is their customers who blend the generic with the necessary ingredients or elements to produce the final capsule, tablet or medicine which is then offered to the retail market. As such manufacturers are not burdened with research, development or marketing costs they are able to offer their products at a fraction of the price of the originals – something which even government agencies have not been slow to appreciate.

It is just a short step from here to true counterfeiting and the rewards are much greater. By printing packaging bearing another company's name and logo the infringer can offer this product at a price closer to that of the original and very much more than the generic alone. This happened in the Pfizer Mecadox case in 1978. Product counterfeiting can damage a company financially but the possibility of a subsequent, unfounded product liability writ is of far greater concern to the pharmaceutical industry than simply the loss of revenues and profits.

VIDEO PIRACY

The film industry has always had to face the challenge of piracy but in the late 1970s it experienced a phenomenal increase in the activities of those who chose to ignore its property rights – it was the advent of video piracy. Prior to this time reproducing celluloid film was expensive and technically difficult. Suddenly the home video enabled anyone to record films illegally, lend them to friends or rent them for a fee. It is impossible to calculate accurately the loss to the industry, but according to the Motion Picture Association of America it is believed to exceed $700 million per year. Though the industry has always been active in protecting its rights its procedures proved totally inadequate to deal with the new problems.

The rewards of video piracy were such that organised crime soon took an interest and the industry was suddenly faced with pirates whose methods were reminiscent of the gang wars of the thirties. In addition to the theft of master films from cinemas by armed gangs, it had also to face large-scale organised duplication and export networks. In 1978, the IFPI (International Federation for the Phonograph Industry) was expanded to include video and anti-piracy activities began to take shape. The extent of the problem was worldwide but was particularly serious in the UK and the Netherlands. As a result, in 1982, they established their own anti-piracy groups – the Federation Against Copyright Theft (FACT), and the Stichting Video Veilig. FACT's first Secretary-General was Robert Birch, a former member of Scotland Yard's Legal Department with Peter Duffy, a former Commander of Scotland Yard's Anti-Terrorist Group as Operations Director. FACT soon made its presence felt and by working with the authorities was able to achieve a high level of success.

Unlike other forms of commercial counterfeiting, in the UK video piracy has always been subject to the criminal law. Apart from the trademark offences connected with the copying of labels, etc., the duplicating of film is an offence under the Copyright Act. It carried, unfortunately, only a nominal fine and the police were never keen on prosecuting such cases. FACT lobbied

Parliament and was instrumental in having the 1956 Copyright Act amended to cope with these new problems. To be in possession of pirate video film and sound recordings for trade now carries strong penalties. These amendments are limited, however, as they only relate to the needs of the video and audio industries.

In the United States special sections were established within the FBI to liaise with the film industry and its regulatory and policing bodies and in most European countries laws have been strengthened, or introduced, to enable the authorities to deal with this new criminal activity. The lesson to be learned from the video industry is that by working together, sharing one's resources and information and presenting a unified front considerable progress can be made in the fight against the counterfeiter.

DO YOU HAVE A PROBLEM?

Manufacturers frequently have difficulty in establishing whether or not their products are being copied. The first clue often comes when a member of the public returns a product or lodges a complaint. Amazingly, however, few companies conduct the most elementary tests to verify the authenticity of returned merchandise. If the product is a watch or camera, its origins are quickly recognised. When dealing with articles such as perfumes, cosmetics or clothes, they are frequently replaced with a standard letter of apology. Sometimes the returned merchandise is forwarded to the production plant for examination but mostly it is considered natural wastage and merely written off. One British company, over an eighteen-month period, had more than twenty articles returned as faulty without realising that none of them was genuine. The first hint of counterfeiting was provided by another member of the public who reported that the quality of the paintwork was so poor it could not be genuine!

Many companies never consider the possibility that the fault may not be theirs. The idea that the articles could be copied never occurs to them. Such carelessness is dangerous. Every returned product should be thoroughly examined not only to identify the faults but also to check that the article is genuine. Companies should also pay attention to trade rumours that products are being copied. Such rumours may prove to be just that, but who can afford to ignore them?

One of the largest cases involving counterfeit jeans started as a rumour and it was only after months of investigation that the first bogus garments were discovered. Subsequently, it was proved that thousands of garments had been manufactured and shipped to the Middle East, where they were sold to site workers. It was only when the goods began to be sold in retail outlets in Europe that direct evidence was obtained.

INFORMANTS

Another frequent occurrence is the appearance of an informant. He arrives unannounced and is prepared to disclose all for a price. At that stage you may not be aware that you even have a problem, but now you do. What action should be taken?

The use of informants can be extremely precarious. The results can be disappointing or positively dangerous to one's case and a waste of money. That is not to say that such informants should be ignored, merely that their use should be carefully controlled and supervised. The informant should be bound by a legal agreement and only paid when the case has been prosecuted.

Informants should be asked to produce positive evidence to support their claims and this initial evidence must be more substantial than mere artwork or test phials of perfume, both of which can easily be used to defraud an alleged victim. Demand evidence that can only be produced as part of a production run and at considerable expense, such as counterfeit bottles or metal fittings.

If you are satisfied that you have a problem and that your informant could be of assistance, you must then decide who can best deal with him. Ideally the matter should be handed over to your lawyer or to an investigator. They must ensure that all the facts are properly evaluated and presented in a usable form. They must verify the evidence and complete the evidential chain.

Be aware too that the use of informants can sometimes have an adverse effect. If a case is taken to court on informant evidence alone, expect some criticism. The defence will claim that he is a bought witness and was party to the actual conspiracy. This may discredit him as a witness and result in the court looking with disfavour on the entire case.

LEGAL REMEDIES

In the fourteenth century an innkeeper found guilty of passing off an inferior wine as a Rudesheimer was ordered by the Elector Palatine to be hanged. In sixteenth-century England and France, the penalty for counterfeiting was death. In 1597, two goldsmiths in England who were found guilty of making and selling gold plate of less than the marked quality were sentenced to be nailed to the pillory by their ears.

Today's civil remedies, though less robust, can still be reasonably effective but implementation can be expensive and frustrating, and criminal legislation is certainly in need of considerable reform if it is to be effective against commercial counterfeiting. The advantages of using the criminal law are the saving of court costs and the assistance which can be given by the police, Customs and other official bodies. The main criminal remedies in England and Wales are contained within the Trade Descriptions Act, the Copyright Act and the offences of deception under the Theft Act. The common law offence of Conspiracy to Defraud can also be used by the police when dealing with these cases. It should be noted, however, that where the conspiracy is to be carried out abroad it is not indictable in England even if its performance would cause economic loss and damage to the proprietary interests of a British company. The Trade Descriptions Act 1968 has also proved quite effective and Trading Standards Officers have had much success, but the Act is still somewhat limited.

In the United States the Trademark Counterfeiting Act is proving invaluable for those engaged in prosecuting piracy.

Another useful weapon is the Organised Crime Control Act (The Racketeer Influenced and Corrupt Organisation Act – RICO). For an action to succeed under the provisions of RICO the plaintiffs must prove one of four specific activities:

(1) Mail fraud
(2) Wire fraud
(3) Interstate transportation of stolen property
(4) Receiving stolen property transported interstate

It would be impossible for a commercial counterfeiting conspiracy to function without committing either, or both, of the first two offences and therefore the provisions of RICO can frequently be invoked. Unfortunately, there appears to be a reluctance on the part of victims to make full use of this legislation. The idea that one is up against racketeers when dealing with counterfeiters has proved frightening to many complainants.

On occasions counterfeiters have been forewarned of a pending legal action, enabling him to deprive the plaintiffs of the evidence that had earlier been available and without which the case would be in jeopardy. It is therefore essential that the pirate's counterfeit merchandise, his machinery, if unique to the operation, and his books and records are seized to prevent their removal or destruction. This need has now been acknowledged by the courts and we have a valuable addition to the armoury against counterfeiting – the Seizure Order. The actual number of such orders currently issued is not known, but within the United Kingdom and the United States their use has become routine. Seizure Orders have their counterparts in Europe and elsewhere. The essential element of such orders is that one must first satisfy the courts that an order is necessary to prevent the destruction, or removal, of essential evidence. The British Order takes its name from a stated case and is known as the Anton Pillar Order. It can also be extended to include a requirement that defendants must disclose their sources of supply, customers, and so on. However, these powerful orders are not without their critics – both within and outside the judiciary.

The legal basis of the American Seizure Order is now contained within the Trademark Conterfeiting Act which authorises a court to direct seizure and impoundment of all infringing merchandise in a defendant's possession, custody or control. The need for such an order was typified in the notorious

Vuitton et Fils SA versus Crown Handbags case which took place in the United States during 1980. In that case Vuitton, after perusing the defendant's records, was unable to find any evidence demonstrating what portion, if any, of the revenues reflected in those records was derived from the sale of counterfeit Vuitton products. As a result the courts awarded Vuitton costs based only on the offer for sale of six counterfeit bags by the defendants to Vuitton's own private investigator. This was a ridiculous state of affairs but, without direct evidence, there was no way of knowing whether the defendants had sold six, 600 or 6 million counterfeit articles.

In the UK and the US such orders allow the plaintiff, or his agent, to be present during their execution but in other countries orders are usually served by a court official. For example, in France a *saisie* can officially only be executed by a *huissier*, or bailiff. This can present problems as the court official may not always be familiar with the ramifications of the case and consequently may fail to appreciate the significance of records seen but not seized. In Belgium, the bailiff can be pre-selected by the plaintiff and briefed in advance but mistakes can and do occur.

In an Anton Pillar action, the order is served by the plaintiff's solicitors but his investigator, usually the person who actually conducted the enquiries, or his client's technical expert, can be present. The American Orders are dealt with by Customs officials and the United States Marshals.

Seizure Orders have proved invaluable in the fight against commercial counterfeiting and they have helped redress the balance in favour of the plaintiff, though the pirate still remains in the lead.

INVESTIGATIONS

The involvement of professional criminals in commercial counterfeiting has meant that the investigation of these conspiracies has necessarily become more complex. It is now quite normal for the counterfeiters to:

— deal exclusively in cash;
— maintain no records of either purchases of sales of the products;
— secrete their stocks of counterfeit goods;
— use innocent persons to front their operations;
— obtain their raw materials or components from various countries, carry out assembly in others, and sell in yet others;
— deliver their products unlabelled, sending the packaging and/or labels by post, thus leaving the customer to assemble the finished article.

Consequently, the pursuit of those responsible must be planned and handled with patience and skill. Premature action merely drives the principals underground and allows them to emerge elsewhere at a later date. Once a criminal group realises the profits to be made from commercial counterfeiting they are reluctant to give them up and it takes more than the payment of fines or damages to cool their enthusiasm. Even the threat of imprisonment may not be a deterrent.

PARALLEL TRADING

All the major perfume houses have exclusive distribution networks and consequently less exclusive outlets are always seeking to sell their products. Also, pricing structures can vary so much between countries (due, for example, to changing exchange rates), that it can be economically viable to purchase in one country, sell in another, and still undercut the officially appointed agent. This is known as 'parallel trading' and is perfectly legal. It provides, however, a perfect 'grey' market into which counterfeiters can move their products.

The 'grey' market is of tremendous concern to all manufacturers of branded goods whether their merchandise be drinks, clothes, foods or motor spares. It covers the entire spectrum of products and can seriously threaten a company's international operations. Within such 'common markets' as the European Economic Community this trade is encouraged. For example, Article 85(1) of the Treaty of Rome prohibits any agreements which restrict competition and threaten the unity of the Common Market. Those cartels set up before the Second World War, whereby all producers in an industry fixed prices and decided markets by quota, are clearly in contravention. But the problem lies not so much with Article 85(1) as with Article 38. Free movement of goods within the EEC is an important principle, but when pricing structures are distorted by exchange rates, price controls (the bane of the pharmaceutical industry) and other non-equivalent conditions, parallel trading becomes possible and profitable. The EEC Commission thus encourages free movement and parallel trade, even for pharmaceutical goods. Companies are therefore caught between their wish to control their distribution and the Treaty of Rome. Manufacturers are unable adequately to control their distribution arrangements and a 'grey' market has arisen which counterfeiters are able to take advantage of, frequently by mixing counterfeit products in with genuine ones.

Counterfeiters are assisted by the fact that:

— traders assume that cheap goods are genuine but originate 'abroad' and do not therefore bother to check authenticity;
— the low prices of counterfeit products do not attract particular attention;
— a distribution network exists where brokers do not ask questions.

Companies cannot afford to ignore this 'grey' market – it is an area which, unless closely monitored, can result in a brand's total collapse.

PRACTICAL STEPS

Secret marks on products, the addition of tracers to chemicals, deliberate flaws in stitching on clothing are all steps which manufacturers can take so as to identify their own products readily. But to be of value, knowledge of their existence must be restricted to only a few people. If they become common knowledge pirates will duplicate them on their counterfeit products. Having marked your merchandise make frequent but irregular test purchases, particularly of products in the 'grey' market. Remember that pirates make a regular habit of mixing counterfeits with genuine articles. Companies should also develop product protection strategies. These should define exactly what to do in the event of their products being counterfeited. Should the sales personnel be informed? Who should conduct the investigation? To whom should the investigator report? Consider too the use of public warnings, and even invite the public to assist you in your fight against piracy. Suitably worded notices can have a tremendous affect on your campaign, as demonstrated by Levi Strauss, United Features Syndicate (with Snoopy), Pfizer and many others.

MUTUAL AID GROUPS

Learn too from the experiences of others. Discuss your possible problems with companies whose products have actually been copied. By sharing knowledge and information much can be achieved.

The most active group is the International Anti-Counterfeiting Coalition (IACC). This is a voluntary body which was established in 1978. It is based in San Francisco but has members throughout the world. It combats product counterfeiting by co-operation with law enforcement agencies and by mutual assistance. It is also active in lobbying governments and regulatory authorities. It was this group which was instrumental in drawing up the International Anti-Counterfeiting Code. Within the United States its lobbying resulted in the enactment of the Trademark Counterfeiting Act, 1984.

An International Anti-Counterfeiting Code was suggested to GATT in 1982 by the governments of the EEC and the United States and, if adopted, would enable trademark owners, or their agents, to seek the assistance of the public authorities in all signatory countries – 'to intercept and enforce forfeiture of all shipments of counterfeit merchandise seeking customs clearance'. This is a welcome development but unless trademark owners can specifically identify the vessel bringing the counterfeit products into the country, or identify the port or airport being used, then the code will not be effective.

The British equivalent of the IACC is the Anti-Counterfeiting Group (ACG). Its basic objectives are the same as those of its international counterpart but the ACG, for reasons best known to itself, cloaks its operations in secrecy; IACC, on the other hand, publicises its aims, its membership and its successes.

The International Chambers of Commerce are also active in anti-counterfeiting and in Italy, the European home of counterfeiting, a group of Italian and Italian-based French companies have established their own intelligence operation, COLC. Exchange of information and the co-ordination of proceedings are high on their list of priorities.

CONCLUSIONS

Counterfeiting is a profitable and growing activity which poses a serious threat to manufacturers of branded products. It is frequently very well funded and organised and is prevalent in virtually every market in the world. Unfortunately, brand owners are frequently their own worst enemies. They often fail to take even the most elementary precautions to protect their brands and even where clear evidence of counterfeiting exists manufacturers sometimes choose to ignore it. Fortunately this attitude is changing and brand owners are becoming more vigilant, but the battle has yet to be won.

7 Developing New Brands

TOM BLACKETT
GRAHAM DENTON

WHY DO COMPANIES NEED NEW PRODUCTS?

We live in a dynamic and rapidly changing world. Increased leisure time, more 'working mothers', cheaper travel and the explosion of mass communications have all caused consumers to re-examine their life-styles and aspirations and thus have created new patterns of demand. So now, more than ever before, companies need successful new products:

— to replace the volume and profits from established products either under attack from competitors, or nearing the end of their life-cycles;
— to develop their business by seizing fresh opportunities to satisfy consumer demand.

Whatever the purpose, successful new product development, under increasingly complex and competitive conditions, has become a hazardous, expensive business. The risk of failure is high – eight out of ten new products fail to make the grade – and the cost of failure in cash, labour, sales force morale, trade and consumer prestige is often substantial. Few companies, therefore, can afford to sustain investment in new product development without a reasonable chance of success. But, equally, few companies nowadays can confidently anticipate corporate growth without new products.

So what can be done to help reduce the high element of risk inherent in new product development? What can be done to promote the chances of success?

WHAT MAKES NEW PRODUCTS SUCCESSFUL?

The London based research consultancy NOP recently conducted a survey of sixty-two major UK manufacturers. They asked the executives responsible for new product development in each company to say why their last successful new product had done well. Table 7.1 summarises responses to this question and the results suggest that product differentiation (a 'unique selling proposition' or USP) is of prime importance as is the need to gain a high level of trade acceptance.

TABLE 7.1 *Reasons for the success of a new product*

	Total	Food and drink manufacturers	Others
(Base-respondents)	(62)	(34)	(28)
	%	%	%
Product had a 'USP'	58	56	61
High level of trade acceptance	47	44	50
High level of 'above the line' investment	44	41	47
Performance advantage over competition	44	27	64

NOP also asked what were the main reasons for failure, and the reasons given are shown in Table 7.2. Once again trade influence is shown to be important, though the absence of a USP emerges as the most influential single factor.

TABLE 7.2 *Reasons for the failure of a new product*

	Total	Food and drink manufacturers	Others
(Base-respondents)	(62)	(34)	(28)
	%	%	%
No 'USP'	37	32	43
Trade resistance	32	35	29
Inadequate trial	27	24	32
Inadequate repeat purchasing	27	29	25
No quality advantage	18	18	18

Finally, when asked to review performance over the last five years and to say what factors were thought to have discriminated most between success and failure with new products (Table 7.3), product quality, especially in food and drinks, and the existence of a USP emerged as the most important factors.

In order to be successful, therefore, new products must offer a blend of quality and distinctiveness. They must offer consumers distinct and credible benefits that are relevant to their requirements, are desirable and are

TABLE 7.3   *Discriminating factors in the success or failure of a new product*

	Total	Food and drink manufacturers	Others
(Base-respondents)	(62)	(34)	(28)
	%	%	%
Product quality	53	65	39
Uniqueness of product	44	41	47
Level of trade acceptance	39	44	32
Level of advertising investment	36	35	36
Level of distribution achieved	32	35	29
Price	31	38	21
Company commitment	24	24	25
Sales force motivation	23	29	14

influential upon the purchase decision. We call this quality 'the significant point of difference'.

THE ESSENTIAL NEED FOR A 'POINT OF DIFFERENCE'

It seems extraordinary that so many 'new' products launched on the market patently lack a significant point of difference. According to Marketing Intelligence Service, a US new products intelligence company, 90 per cent of all 'new' products introduced in North America in the last fifteen years were not really new at all. They were new sizes, new packaging variations, new formulations, new flavours, but not new products. This, of course, is low risk innovation, a safety-first approach designed to sustain or revive interest in products coming under competitive pressure or reaching maturity.

Imitation too is often a temptation manufacturers find difficult to resist. 'Why not let your competitor take the risks in building a new market' the argument runs 'and then, when consumer awareness and interest is at a peak, launch your own version of his product?' This also is in theory low-risk innovation; but the theory, as Colgate-Palmolive found in the United States, can be confounded by reality:

Cue toothpaste. It was a perfectly good product. The only problem was that Cue had no significant point of difference from Crest, which was already a market leader for P. & G. Our main reason for launching Cue was to threaten Crest which, as it turned out, had little to worry about since we wound up losing $15 million in just one year.

David R. Foster, Past President Colgate-Palmolive Company

So the golden rule for developing successful new products is always to offer a significant point of difference. But before we discuss how you can make sure your product offers one let us talk about the ideas behind the products and – most importantly – the planning behind the ideas.

SETTING THE NEW PRODUCT STRATEGY

Why is it that companies like Procter and Gamble, IBM, Pedigree Petfoods, Unilever and Nabisco appear so consistently good at innovation? Why are products launched by these companies so frequently nominated as 'best new brands of the year' by retailers and consumers? The answer is quite simple: all these companies recognise how important new products are to their corporate development and all have organised themselves accordingly.

From their 1982 survey of management attitudes and practices in new product development, consultants Booz Allen & Hamilton concluded that the most successful innovators tend to be those companies with a formalised development process to which a consistent commitment is made in terms of financial resources, staffing and senior management support. On the basis of this survey, Booz Allen developed the following set of 'best practices' for companies seeking to improve new product performance:

— define the role that new products are required to play in your corporate growth programme
— make the long-term commitment necessary to support innovation and new product development
— establish an environment – a management style, organisational structure and degree of top-management support – conducive to developing 'company-specific' new products
— capitalise on accumulated experience to achieve and maintain competitive advantage

And above all:
— develop and implement a 'company-specific' approach, driven by corporate objectives, with a well-defined new product strategy at its core.

Successful new products rarely evolve through haphazard processes or 'chance encounters'. They evolve through careful analysis of existing markets and emerging consumer trends, of internal company resources and capabilities, of management styles and of new product experience. Such analysis identifies markets for which new products can be developed and suggests the internal criteria that must be met in order to ensure that the new product process is linked to wider corporate growth objectives. This, Booz Allen concludes, is the essence of a good new product strategy, it 'links the new product process to company objectives and provides focus for idea/concept generation'.

But what of the ideas themselves, how are these generated? Let us examine some of the more commonly used sources.

THE MAIN SOURCES OF NEW PRODUCT IDEAS

A few years ago, the *Journal of Marketing* (August 1979) reported:

> To produce a single successful new product, 80 ideas are required; 85 per cent of scientists' and engineers' development time is spent on products failing on introduction. Of every ten products that emerge from Research and Development, half fail in product and market tests, and only two become commercial successes.

And in his book, *New Product Development Strategies* (1981) Frederick D. Buggie advised: 'Generate as many possible answers (to the new product problem) as you can. The larger your pool of possibilities the more likely that a winner or two will be among them.'

It is tempting to speculate then that the wider the net is cast in search of new product ideas the greater is the chance of ultimate success. Provided your new product strategy is clearly defined and the exploratory process is guided by agreed and 'company-specific' parameters then this is almost certainly true. But the sources of new product ideas are numerous; let us look at just a few:

(1) creative flair, including anyone from the Chairman's wife to the boy in the post room at the advertising agency:
(2) Research and Development breakthroughs;
(3) formal search procedures, including foreign market intelligence, the scientific and trade press, 'segmentation analysis' of markets and structured consumer investigations;
(4) deliberate invention, including 'brainstorming' with company employees and professional advisers, focus groups among consumers and Synectic techniques.

So which approach – or combination of approaches – is likely to work best for you? In the final analysis it depends upon the nature of the market you intend to enter. In high-technology 'sunrise' industries, for instance, the importance of R&D excellence linked to creative flair is paramount. As an executive of a major US corporation told Booz Hamilton:

> We are trying to develop innovations that will reach the market in five to ten years. Our new product development executives understand today's market

place, but they emphasise technology to generate new product ideas since they have no mechanism to identify the market requirements five to ten years from now.

Alternatively in mature, well-structured consumer markets the situation is often very different. Here new product ideas are increasingly consumer based and dependent upon careful qualitative and quantitative surveys of attitudes and behaviour, searches of overseas markets and exploratory work with 'creative consumers'. And it is in markets like these, where the whole 'art' of successful new product marketing is infinitely more subtle, that the need to differentiate your product offering – to offer a 'significant point of difference' – has become essential.

CAPTURING THE 'POINT OF DIFFERENCE'

So what is a significant point of difference – and how can you be sure that your new product offers one? There are five basic guidelines:

A significant point of difference must be
— recognisable by consumers;
— desirable;
— based on an element of familiarity;
— credible on delivery;
— communicated in every aspect of presentation.

First, a significant point of difference must be one that consumers can *recognise*. This sounds obvious, but too many new products tend to be based on technical differences, measurable in the laboratory, but not obvious to the consumer. An example of this is the cake mix Moist & Easy from Procter & Gamble in the United States. 'Moistness' is believed to be the Holy Grail in cake mix terms and Moist & Easy was technically more moist than the competition, Betty Crocker's Snackin Cake. However, when consumers tasted it in 'blind' tests it performed disappointingly. Despite this Procter & Gamble launched the product. Some seven years later Moist & Easy was withdrawn in America and absorbed, as a variety, within the Duncan Hines flavour line in Canada. Moist & Easy was a failure, its assumed technical superiority was unable to make up for its deficiencies in taste.

It is important, therefore, that new products should be thoroughly and sensitively researched to make sure that consumers recognise the point of difference and that it matters to them.

Next, a significant point of difference must be one that consumers *need* or *want*; and what do consumers need or want? They want benefits like:

(1) quality, as endorsed by brand names they have learned to trust;
(2) improved performance, as with the first soft margarines which were much

easier to spread, especially straight from the fridge;

(3) value, as with supermarket own-brands and generic products;

(4) convenience, as with sheet fabric conditioners which work in the dryer, thus doing away with the need to catch the rinse cycle with a liquid;

(5) solutions to problems, as with the first fluoride toothpastes which significantly reduced dental decay;

(6) new services, such as 'Breakfast at McDonalds', a fast, wholesome and inexpensive breakfast for busy people.

If your new product is not needed or not wanted it will not be significant. However, consumers do not always know what they need or want – and that is especially true when it comes to new products. And this takes us to our third guideline.

A significant point of difference must go hand in hand with an *element of familiarity*, which should highlight the point of difference, or originality, by contrasting with it. For example, underlined is the element of familiarity for each of these once-new products:

— Liquid Soap

— Spray Polish

— Diet Soft Drinks

— Disposable Razors

— Aerosol Cream

— Dry Roast Peanuts

— Paper Towels

— Light Beer

Consumers are more perceptive to a new product when they can see a chord of familiarity, something that links it to their past experience.

And next, a significant point of difference must have *credibility which is confirmed on delivery*. Consumers must believe that the new product will deliver the significant point of difference it promises. If they do not believe, they will not make a first purchase; and if you do not deliver, they will not buy again. For example, the significant point of difference for the US brand Ultra Max Shampoo was that it was a shampoo specially formulated for people who blow-dry their hair. Ultra Max got a trial because consumers found the point of difference credible – but as soon as they realised that it was no better than their regular shampoos for blow-drying, they stopped buying. Ultra Max offered a point of difference that was credible but not delivered. Therefore, it was not significant – and Ultra Max failed.

Finally, a significant point of difference must be *communicated in every aspect of presentation*. Presentation covers every element that could express the point of difference: that means the brand name, pack, price, the product itself, its appeal and ultimately its promotion. Presentation defines the consumer proposition of a new product, communicating the point of difference and establishing the brand identity. Indeed branding, in the presentation of an idea, can in itself often create a new product's point of difference. Here are three examples where that phenomenon occurred:

(1) L'Eggs pantyhose, a unique presentation in terms of package, name and merchandising through racks. The pantyhose were no better or worse than any other brand – yet in the United States the brand has been a huge success.

(2) Clinique cosmetics, a totally new presentation for cosmetics: skin care rather than skin beautification. An appropriate, therapeutic name, packaging to match, and an incredibly successful brand on both sides of the Atlantic.

(3) Tic Tac mints, a new name and pack that put more mints in your pockets at higher profit than any of us would have thought logically possible.

Branding is therefore crucial because people buy brands not products. People do not buy shaving cream, they buy Gillette Foamy, Old Spice or even a can of the store's own-brand shaving cream. In fact, we have become so inured to brands that even generic brands are brands in the consumer's mind. That is why we firmly believe that in the new product development process you should concentrate on developing new brands, not just new products, because brands can offer consumers a significant point of differernce.

So, if the five golden rules of developing successful new brands are so simple, why is it that the failure rate continues to be unacceptably high? Frequently it is because companies fail to understand how their new product's point of difference can be significant to consumers.

UNDERSTANDING HOW BRANDS APPEAL

A point of difference can appeal in one or more of four ways. These appeals are best illustrated by looking at how people are aware. Since the time of Plato it has been widely believed that people are aware in four ways. This understanding of the four kinds of awareness was used by Jung in his teaching on human psychology. He gave the four functions of the mind specific names:

— *thinking*, which deals with logic and rationale;
— *sensation*, which is the direct perception of phenomena;
— *feeling*, which is concerned with emotions;
— *intuition*, which is the ability to sense the intangible in a situation.

We are aware in all these four ways. We are open to four kinds of appeal and this means that brands can appeal in a number of ways. It also means that new brands have four key ways in which to be distinct from competition.

Consumer products normally employ a combination of appeals but in their positioning and presentation are usually led by one primary appeal. So, because some brands focus more on one type of appeal and some on another, we need more than one model to understand how new brands can be successful.

First, rational appeals. It is sometimes said that man is a rational animal and certainly there are many rational brands on sale. For years now Procter & Gamble has built huge businesses on tangible points of difference which are demonstrated in a logical way. These are rational brands: Crest helps prevent cavities; Tide washes whiter; Bounce is more convenient because you do not have to rush for the rinse cycle. And rational appeals also crop up in other markets: the appeal of low tar or mild cigarettes is fundamentally rational – as is the appeal of low calorie tonic water, lead-free petrol and disposable lighters.

Secondly, sensation. Virtually all food brands appeal to the senses; for many it is the primary appeal which the brand has to make. If the ketchup did not taste good there would be little reason to buy it. Freshen-Up, a liquid centre gum in the United States, offers a distinct sensation in the mouth with its mint centre. However, Pringles, the formed potato crisp, made little appeal to the senses – its flavour was remorselessly bland, unvarying and predictable, its shape and texture uniform. Consumers like Pringles – but not enough. It failed to set the snack food market on fire. But sensation-based brands are not limited to foods. Pears Soap in the United Kingdom employs a sensation-based point of difference with its highly distinctive fragrance.

Thirdly, emotional appeals. We react to the world with more than logic, we react with emotion. We make value judgements and become deeply committed for or against something. New York Life, a life insurance company, creates an emotional aura around the insurance it sells; we see the values we cherish – family, children, future financial security – held up for approval. Virtually everyone in the target audience endorses these values and feels to some extent committed to the same aims as the advertiser. Contrast this with the advertising for Cointreau liqueur: here an overt yet restrained sexuality reinforces the sensual properties of the brand – but the light-hearted fantasy prevents any embarrassment among the essentially middle-class target audience.

Fourthly, intuitive appeals. We react to the world with intuition in even more ways than with sensation, logic and emotion. Much of what we do is intuitive; it is the skill that aids judgement – and without intuition, none of us would hire a secretary, choose a restaurant for dinner or find a path through a maze of apparently conflicting information. Somehow we just know that we should be following a certain direction. There are lots of intuitive brands which we know instinctively are brands for people like us, brands which fit our life-styles. Intuitive brands are the stuff of everyday, they help us convey something about ourselves to the world at large. Intuitive brands are different from the emotion-led brands which stir us and touch a chord that moves us deeply.

If you like, emotion-led brands are introverted and intuitive brands are extroverted. Marlboro advertising conveys a point about intuitive-led brands – the cowboy, the West, the mythology says it all. Another example is beer; what is the difference between Miller and Budweiser? Apart from minor differences in formulation, the main difference is that different people feel comfortable with different brands. So, intuitive brands enable consumers to say something about themselves. Consumers identify with intuitive brands and make a personal statement about themselves when they buy. Such intuitive appeals are a tremendous asset for a brand.

But how do we make certain that the new product is offering a significant point of difference that appeals to people? How do we hear the consumer's final say before investing millions in a new product? In other words, how do we increase our odds of being right? The answer lies in the research.

KEEPING THE RESEARCH HONEST

All too often, however, research fails to produce the right answers – it says go when it should say stop, and it says stop when it should say go. There are five maxims to keep the new product research honest:

(1) test new products *alongside competitive* products;
(2) identify and test *key differences*;
(3) establish who is your *target market* (these are usually heavy buyers of key competitors) and conduct your testing accordingly;
(4) get to the bottom of *consumer motivation*;
(5) use *realistic consumer stimuli*.

To illustrate the first maxim let us take a hypothetical example: 'This new 3-ply toilet tissue is extra soft and strong, and costs $1.44 for four rolls.' This is a typical new product concept statement, a typewritten statement on a card. It achieved favourable consumer reaction in Canada and the United States but the product failed in each country after considerable test market expenditure. Research had given the wrong answer: it had said go when it should have said stop. So how could the research have been designed to give the right answer? Well, if a 3-D presentation had been shown alongside the existing market place competition, consumers would have seen the new product as too expensive. The new product gave fewer sheets per dollar and in this market economy and value for money matter as much as softness and strength.

So you should always test new products alongside competitive products. But *what* exactly should you test? Companies often fail to identify the key variables in their new product proposition, and they end up testing the wrong things. For instance, if you are developing a new cigarette, taste and satisfaction are only part of the story. You need to test the image of the new product *vis-à-vis* competitors since this is where the difference will lie. And if you are developing a perfume, the accompanying fantasies and user image are more important variables than the fragrance itself. But if you are developing a new cereal for children, fun and size-impression are key – and these are the variables that should be tested.

The third maxim concerns the nature of the consumer 'sample' you should use for your new product research. Taking an example from the confectionery market, if you carry out your research among a representative mix of heavy and light buyers of candy bars you might find that the majority opinion tends to favour 'a new taste sensation' when it comes to new product requirements. But if you consider carefully, there is often an important difference between what heavy and light users want. Light users – the majority in this and in most markets – may well want a new taste sensation; heavy users, however, could want something very different – value or a longer lasting bar, for example. And in this market the 'heavies' (perhaps literally!) account for 80 per cent of the volume. All too often market researchers recruit all users and therefore submerge the critical opinion of the minority. You must identify your target market and pay attention to what the heavy user has to say. To do this you must listen to consumers, interpret what they have to say about your new product, about competition and about the market. In other words, you must probe and cross-examine, you must get to the bottom of consumer motivation.

Consumers themselves, however, cannot analyse their motivation, they cannot put their motivations into an order of importance. That is the researcher's job and it is best approached indirectly. For instance, let us assume you want to find out why motorists go to specialist exhaust replacement shops like Kwikfit or Midas instead of to local garages. If you ask a direct question like 'Why do you go to Midas?' you get an easy, logical answer like 'Because they're quick and efficient'. A logical answer like this makes the respondent feel good because he or she has answered the question – and it makes the researcher feel good because it is simple to pass on to the client. But it is the wrong answer.

Alternatively if you ask the same people an indirect question such as 'What were your feelings the last time you took your car for repair at a garage?' you get an answer like 'I was afraid' or 'They put a hammer through a perfectly good exhaust' or 'It was a rip-off'. Through this type of comment you discover that the real advantage of the specialist exhaust shop is predictable cost or, even, honesty.

The principle of directive questioning is applied to quantitative as well as to qualitative research. So you dig deeper and ask respondents to rate their local garage against such attributes as friendliness, price and honesty. You then analyse these results against those of respondents who do use an exhaust shop. You find that they agree that the local garage was friendly and had good prices

– but their views differ on the subject of honesty. Thus you discover that the real advantage of the exhaust shop over the garage is the perception of honesty.

The final maxim concerns speaking to consumers in a way they understand. Too many good ideas are lost because of the way they are presented to consumers. You would not speak Chinese to an Italian and expect him to understand, so it does not make sense to speak to the consumer in marketing or research jargon. Do not show unresolved hypotheses, show things that look like advertisements or television commercials, or look or sound like radio spots. Develop proposition boards that look like real press advertisements. Portray the idea clearly and explicitly but do not sell it. This format provides consumers with something to relate to, something familiar, and in this way we can test alternative approaches, especially emotional and intuitive ones, with greater care. Show consumers comprehensive 3-dimensional pack designs too because consumers experience great difficulty in visualising a finished, branded package. But whatever you show consumers, make sure it is in a form they can recognise and in a language they can understand.

CONCLUSIONS

Corporate growth, for any firm in any industry, is now increasingly dependent upon successful new products. Successful new product marketing, however, carries high risks – but these can be reduced by adopting a systematic and organised approach. So relate your new product development efforts to specific company objectives, analyse your corporate strengths and weaknesses, resources and capabilities and define your new product objectives accordingly. Construct a new product strategy. Commit staff and financial resources to the fulfilment of your strategy but accept that successful NPD is rarely achieved overnight. Consider all possible sources of new product ideas, recognise that some may be more applicable to your business than others but disdain none.

Above all, remember that the main reason new products fail is because they lack distinctiveness. Seek, therefore, to develop ideas into products which, in their formulation, packaging, branding and general appeal offer a 'significant point of difference', a point of difference that is:

— recognisable by consumers;
— relevant to their needs or wants;
— based on an 'element of familiarity';
— true to its 'promise';
— communicated in all aspects of presentation.

The best and most successful new products invariably possess these characteristics. Achieving them is never easy and requires significant invest-

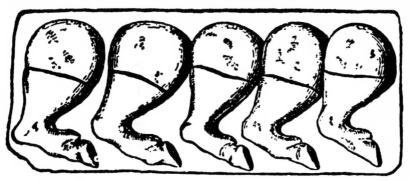

2.1 A Roman sign found at Pompeii. The hams identify a butcher's shop.

Hog in Armour

a

King's Porter and Dwarf

b

Barley Mow

c

The Ape

d

Three Squirrels

e

Bull and Mouth

f

Man in the Moon

g

Hole in the Wall
"A Guide for Malt Worms"

h

Goose and Gridiron

i

Harrow and Doublet

j

2.2 A selection of seventeenth-century English inn signs, with the names shown pictorially.

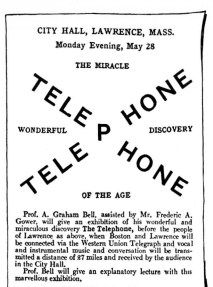

2.3

2.4

2.8

2.5   2.6   2.7

2.3 The first advertisement for the telephone (1887) the year after Bell invented it. Many brand names of the period were similarly classical.

2.4 Early promotion of Camp Coffee with the brand name dominant and emphatic.

2.5 The punning 'lance' logo of Lancia. The name is that of the original manufacturer, Vincenzo Lancia.

2.6 The 'Viking' Rover logo representing the prow of a Viking ship and a Viking head.

2.7 The post-war Volkswagen logo, representing the town of manufacture, Wolfsburg.

2.8 The first Coca-Cola ad. appearing in the *Atlanta Journal*, 29 May 1886.

6.1 Opium Perfume by Yves Saint Laurent. The genuine article is on the left, the counterfeit on the right.

6.2 D-C 90. TDK cassette tapes. The genuine article is on the left, the counterfeit on the right.

6.3 Rolls-Royce Motors CD4074 pistons. The genuine article is on the left, the counterfeit on the right.

6.4 Aramis Denim Aftershave and Cologne. The genuine article is on the left, the counterfeit on the right.

6.5 Colgate toothpaste. The genuine article is on the left, the counterfeit on the right.

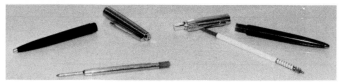

6.6 A Parker ballpoint pen. The genuine article is on the left, the counterfeit is on the right.

6.7 Skate board bearings. The genuine article is on the left, the counterfeit on the right.

6.8 Marshal from Thailand (fake brand), Johnnie Hawker from Indonesia (fake brand), Johnnie Walker Red Label (genuine), Extra Special Old Scotch Whisky (Johnnie Walker black label) (genuine), Extra Special Old Scotch Whisky (Thomas Johnson) from Indonesia (fake brand).

9.1

9.3

9.2

9.1 The Lion Brand uses uses a literal interpretation of the brand name.
9.2 The identity of Lyons Coffee is based strongly on the nature of the product.
9.3 Tactics: an upmarket range of men's toiletries from Shisheido, now one of the world's leading brands in its segment.

9.4a

9.4b

9.4 a and b A common design approach allows Lucas to preserve a strong corporate identity.

(*Left*) 9.5 The ICI symbol acts as a powerful endorsement when used in conjunction with the Dulux House brand.

(*Right*) 9.6 The woodstain imagery reinforces the function of the product.

16.1 A well-organised visual system lends corporate identity clout to all services while retaining individual identities.

16.2a

16.2b

16.2a and b British Airways expresses corporate identity in aircraft livery and interiors. A comprehensive design system extends the corporate personality to include every detail from ticket office to baggage tags.

16.3a

16.3b

16.3 a and b Dramatic change in corporate positioning is effectively communicated by change in corporate 'branding'.

16.4 Brand-dominant companies such as Philip Morris rely almost exclusively on strong individual brands to communicate to the consumer but still need a corporate identity to speak to other groups such as the financial community and governments.

16.5 Regional limitations are dropped with new corporate identity opening new markets and revitalising employee morale.

16.6 Though not a corporate identity, 'Dole', one of Castle & Cook's original brands, was found to have remarkable equity, achieving more than corporate status and maximising synergy across all product lines, categories and sublines.

16.7 A classic example of corporate identity as a new super brand. Stouffer launched in the USA a new line of frozen meals: Lean Cuisine. Introductory costs were kept low by using the equity of the corporate name to presell the consumer without sacrificing excitement or newness.

ment in time and money. We are confident though that provided the commitment is made, such investment will be repaid many times in terms of increased sales and profits.

8 Developing New Brand Names

JOHN M. MURPHY

WHAT'S IN A NAME?

The brand name performs a number of key roles:

— It identifies the product or service, and allows the consumer to specify, reject, or recommend brands.
— It communicates messages to the consumer. In this rôle the name can be either an overt communicator, for example, Draino or Sweet 'n' Low, or a subconscious communicator.
— It functions as a particular piece of legal property in which a manufacturer can sensibly invest and which through law is protected from competitive attack or trespass. Through time and use, a name can become a valuable asset.

The brand name is therefore not only important but is also complex. It must satisfactorily perform a number of quite different roles involving aspects of communication and it also has an important legal role.

STRATEGIC CONSIDERATIONS

In view of the potentially pivotal role that the brand name must frequently play, we are constantly amazed at how often names are selected with little or no real consideration being given to the complex functions they have to perform.

Names selected in such a haphazard fashion, and this applies to company names as well as to product and service names, often turn out to be unsuitable or unprotectable in foreign countries and not infrequently in home markets too! Sometimes they focus too closely on one product benefit or attribute, which over time can become either less important or even detrimental. Or the name is so particular to one product that it actually precludes any form of line

86

extension. Alternatively, the name is too easy for the competition to imitate or, even, improve upon.

What then are the key strategic questions which should be asked early on in the development of brand names?

Is the new product innovative or not?

If the answer is yes, it is probably sensible to develop a name which clearly differentiates the product from its less interesting and innovative competititors. Even if the new product is not particularly innovative there is frequently an opportunity to set it apart from competition by means of an interesting and distinctive brand name.

Is the new product likely to be an international brand in the future?

Strong international brands normally have certain common key characteristics:

— the same brand name in all countries,
— common pack design,
— a broadly similar target market in all countries,
— similar formulation.

Too often brand management is either not aware of plans to market a product on an international scale, or does not consider it sufficiently important to include in a brand name strategy. When this consideration is not taken into account it can later result in loss of time, considerable extra costs, and possible embarrassment and loss of business.

We can all see that fashions are now very similar in London, Paris or New York, whereas fifteen years ago there were wide differences. Middle-class consumers in Thailand are now likely to shop in supermarkets and purchase similar foods to those used by middle-class households in Europe. Well over 50 per cent of all people under the age of 35 in Western Europe speak English, up from 42 per cent in 1969, and less than 25 per cent in 1950. This does not mean that national or cultural differences should be ignored. What is apparent, however, is that the international environment is broadly conducive to international brands, as opposed to local national brands, and is becoming more so. The advantages of international brands can be very real. There are significant promotional 'overlaps' between countries – much American TV is viewed in Canada, many Irish consumers watch British TV, and almost one million Italian adults watch Swiss TV daily. Also strong international brands allow companies to develop strong central co-ordination without fragmenting into a number of semi-autonomous national units. The possibility that your brand might become an international brand obviously should not be ignored.

Is the new product likely to produce line extensions, or to be part of a range?

Line extensions and ranges of products are frequently more effective and less costly methods for introducing new products than adopting separate brand names for each individual product. Through the use of a common brand name, the costs of pack design, brand name development, launch advertising, promotion, and distribution can be sharply reduced.

Again this is an approach which must be carefully considered early on in the development of a naming strategy.

What is the nature of the protection which can be afforded the brand?

If your new product is made by a proprietary process which competitors will be unable to imitate, or if you enjoy a monopoly position, there may be little prospect of competitive brands appearing on the market and therefore descriptive and hence largely unprotectable brand names may be acceptable. If, on the other hand, powerful competitive response is likely an inherently strong and protectable brand name may be essential.

DEVELOPING A BRAND NAME STRATEGY

The strategic considerations involved in developing a brand name strategy are similar to those involved in new product development, positioning or advertising strategy development. Essentially, where brand names are concerned, they involve a series of closely related components:

(1) Product information.
(2) Market information, including competitors, trends, demographics, etc.
(3) Trademark information, including corporate requirements and policies, market place influences, legal requirements, existing company trademarks, etc.
(4) A clear statement of brand objectives based not only on the new product under consideration, but also upon the broader, long-term objectives for the division or the company.

We consider that spending time and effort on these broad strategic branding questions is critical to the development of a strong, appropriate brand name.

(1) Product Information

Product information involves examining carefully the product concept and what the product does; its special properties and its market position; the way it will be used; the satisfaction it brings to the user; its relationship to competitive products; the distribution and media plans; whether the product forms, or will form, part of a range; the points of sale; the 'sex' of the product; the relationship to the company name and to existing trademarks, and so on.

(2) Market Information

Market information involves the gathering together of data relating to the market, both qualitative and quantitative, so that the rôle of the new product and the environment in which it is to be launched is thoroughly understood.

(3) Trademark Information

Trademark information involves establishing those countries, cultures and languages where registration is to be sought, and hence where the name must be particularly appropriate; the message or messages to be communicated by the trademark, and those to be communicated by other means (e.g. advertising and packaging); existing competitive trademarks; any constraints on length; the phonetic qualities sought in the trademark, and the graphic qualities sought.

If, for example, the product in question is an inexpensive toiletry for family use then to give it an expensive, lush name would be inappropriate and discordant. If the product is given too feminine a name it could lead to men rejecting it. If the product is given too 'national' a name (e.g. an Anglo-Saxon, a German, or a French name) it could hinder the creative approach. Again, if the product is innovative it may be sensible to avoid certain well-used word roots such as 'aqua' as this could lead the consumer to believe that the product is similar to the host of other products already on the market. If, on the other hand, the product is positioned as being very similar to existing well established products, it may be sensible to develop trademarks related to the existing 'lexicon'.

The length of the name will also be important. For example, in the case of a toiletry that is to be sold in a bottle which will be displayed upright on the shelf it may be preferable to choose a short word.

(4) Brand Name Objectives

Once one has become familiar with all the available information on the product, the market and on the particular rôle of the trademark, one should set out clearly identified objectives for the naming of the product or service under consideration. We believe that, in addition, these objective should be discussed and agreed by the various levels of management involved in the product – the new product or brand group, senior management, the advertising agency and package designer.

Mutually established and agreed objectives can be a strong unifying element in what can all too frequently become a highly subjective and emotionally charged decision – the choice of a name.

DEVELOPING CREATIVE THEMES

Let us consider the case of a hypothetical Vitamin C tablet. There are a large number of possible themes around which name generation could be centred. For example, names which sound broadly ethical or pharmaceutical in origin could be developed so as to give the product some implied clinical authority; the theme of zest, vitality, energy could be explored, as could a sporting or outdoor theme. Again, a name associated with oranges and fresh fruit, the principal sources of Vitamin C, might be appropriate or a name associated with the countries from which citrus fruits come. It might even be appropriate to suggest through the name a slight aphrodisiac quality – who knows the power of Vitamin C?

In order to choose between these alternative and quite different branding themes, it is important to decide precisely what role the brand name is to play and to relate it to the uses to be made of other means of communication, such as media, advertising and packaging. For example, a sporting name might be inappropriate because the brand name has to 'live' for many years and this particular theme might unduly constrict the media approach in the future. Alternatively, it might be found that in Spain and Italy associations with citrus fruit are inappropriate – citrus fruits could be such a commonplace item of diet as to lend little interest to a brand name for a Vitamin C tablet.

Potential creative themes may well already have emerged from previous qualitative research which can in turn enhance these themes. Certainly in our experience a variety of quite different branding routes are normally available, all of which have varied implications in positioning and differentiating the product.

NAME CREATION

Specialist brand name development companies are increasingly being used to develop both national and international brand names. Such consultants will normally start by examining in detail the company's plans for the new product or service, its marketing objectives and trademark policies and will prepare and agree a naming strategy. Once the brand name development task is clearly defined, work starts on creating new names.

The most productive starting point for the creative process and a useful method for exploring existing themes and searching for possible new ones is the use of carefully selected and managed creative, or focus, groups. For international projects focus groups would be organised on an international basis and each group would be led by a trained psychologist skilled in this area. All members of a particular group are usually of one nationality and are specially chosen for their skills with language. Their task is to develop words, word roots, analogies, phrases and ideas in line with the chosen themes. In the course of a two or three hour creation session a group of six to eight people will create a great mass of verbal raw material – perhaps 500 names in total. Eight or ten such groups may be held and the material produced by the groups would be carefully examined for themes, words, concepts, word roots and associations of significance in the different languages. Copywriters then build up from this consumer-based data an extensive list of potential trademarks – for a typical assignment perhaps 10 000 names or even more.

COMPUTER NAME GENERATION

The qualitative research and focus groups normally provide a clear indication as to the preferred creative themes. For example, the current culture of branding in the volume, executive car area tends to rely on such 'worthy' names as Senator (Opel), Crown (Toyota) and President (Nissan). We have found, however, that our focus groups have indicated a requirement for names with more style and sophistication – after all, when paying a lot of money for an executive car one is buying much more than mobility – one is buying style, peer esteem and a little envy. We have found that 'traditional' executive car names such as President, Senator and Crown are felt by the international creation groups to be altogether too geriatric for the young, dynamic executive and that names with more flair are preferred.

Even though creation groups can provide clear evidence that the current culture of branding in any particular sector is inappropriate or unexciting and fresh creation work can be organised to move along newly defined naming themes, in practice we have found that, in such circumstances, computer techniques can be used productively in three specific areas:

(1) to search existing data bases and computerised dictionaries;
(2) to identify names which possess the required attributes (e.g. masculine, international, stylish, exotic, etc.);
(3) to take existing names and use phonetically based, word-splicing techniques to build new and more interesting names from existing 'core' names.

Many organisations have experimented in the past with computer name generation techniques. It is tempting for firms like Procter & Gamble or

Bristol-Myers to believe that somehow by using a computer to generate names they can effectively reserve for themselves all the good names in any particular sector. In practice, computer name generation programs in the past have tended simply to take vowel/consonant constructions plus some popular letter strings and run all the permutations. Millions of names can be generated in this way but most are totally useless. One major company ran what it thought was a simple program to find a name for a new soft drink. So many names were developed that they estimated one person reading at normal speed for eight hours a day would need four months to go through the output just once!

Mechanistic computer name creation programs are of some limited value in naming pharmaceuticals or chemicals. Most brand names, however, need to have a qualitative element, to be associated in some way with the product or its performance or the satisfactions the product brings. To be useful, therefore, computers need to work within such qualitative parameters and thus need to rely on a database of names coded with reference to the qualities of those names. Computer name generation too needs to take account of natural language, of phonetics and linguistics. Access to computerised synonym and foreign language dictionaries can also greatly enhance the quality of output and assist with name creation.

SELECTING THE NAME

Stage one, therefore, in developing a new brand name is to decide what job you want the new name to perform, now and in the future. Stage two is to isolate those naming themes relevant to the consumer and appropriate in branding and positioning terms. Stage three is to use focus group, copywriters, computers and an existing name library to create names. Since one focus group alone can develop 500 or more potential names, and a short computer run can produce many thousands more, how does one cope with the super-productivity of the creation process?

Brand name development necessarily involves a careful refining process – a great deal of ore has to be fed into the hopper in order to produce a small amount of pure gold – the attractive, strong, protectable brand name. Thus having created a vast list of names it has to be pared down to manageable proportions. To do this, those words are eliminated which at first sight have inherent defects of pronunciation, legibility, memorability or meaning. We also eliminate all those words that are unregistrable as trademarks, which are too close to existing competitive marks or which fail to meet other criteria, e.g. length.

In this way, the initial list of names can be reduced to perhaps one or two hundred candidate names. These would be discussed in detail with our client and a preferred short list of some twenty to thirty names drawn up. Though none of these words would have been checked yet for registrability, they should all appear capable of doing the marketing job in hand.

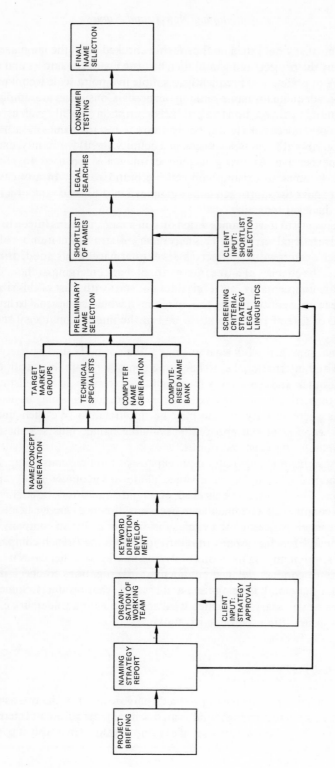

FIGURE 8.1 *The name development process*

This shortlist would then be thoroughly checked in all the languages to be covered by the project, and would then be tested with consumers and ranked according to preference. Frequently, a simple five-point scale technique is, at this stage, adequate for name ranking purposes. Consumers are simply asked to rank the names in relation to a product description on a 'like' versus 'dislike' basis. On other occasions it may be necessary to test the names in rather more depth, e.g. strength versus weakness, masculinity versus femininity, expensive versus inexpensive. Mapping techniques may also be used to relate the shortlisted names to existing competitive brand names. In any case, it is sensible to have the shortlisted names arranged into a broad rank order before starting the legal screening.

Of the twenty to thirty names tested on consumers, perhaps fifteen to twenty will survive to legal screening. This may seem an extravagant number of names but in such overcrowded product classes as pharmaceuticals, food, drinks and cosmetics, the chances of a free international mark emerging at the end of the process are unacceptably low if one does not start with a list of this size. Even with fifteen or twenty carefully chosen names it would be unusual to find more than two or three free marks at the end of the international legal screening process.

The next step then is full legal searching. We normally start by carrying out national and international searches using computer searching facilities. This service is quick and reasonably thorough. We receive a detailed listing of all apparently pertinent marks as well as those where consents may be negotiable or those where validity of title may be questionable. We then undertake detailed searches of the apparently available names plus searches, where appropriate, of unregistered marks.

Such searches and negotiations are expensive and time consuming. It is not uncommon, for example, for a single name to encounter many apparent objections. These must all be checked, often the owners must be contacted and at times commercial agreements are necessary. In once case we helped set up an arrangement whereby the Dutch subsidiary of a British company bought flour from a French company in return for which the French company gave the British company rights to one of its trademarks. In other cases it has been necessary to conduct detailed confidential investigations to check independently if a trademark is being used and if so on what products. Sometimes it may even be necessary to threaten legal action to have a trademark cancelled so as to secure it in a particular country.

IS IT WORTH IT?

The brand name is central to a product's personality. It is the one aspect of a product which never changes and is an essential prerequisite of international marketing. It can become an asset of enormous value. Obviously it pays to get the brand name right, to select one which is legally available in all the countries of interest and to remove all third-party obstacles at relatively low cost before launch, and not at very high cost after launch.

Curiously, however, such a systematic approach is often ignored. Organisations select names with profound marketing and legal defects. They spend fortunes in litigation trying to resolve inherent legal defects. They even, not infrequently, have to withdraw products from the market.

In an age in which companies spend tens, or even hundreds, of millions of dollars or pounds per year advertising and promoting a single product or product line; when the clutter and noise in most sectors increases constantly; when those magical market share points can be worth tens or hundreds of millions of dollars or pounds, the power of the brand name continues to grow. Within the brand name resides all that investment. And it is the only clear, identifiable, aspect of the product that the consumer uses in selection and purchase. Can we afford not to do it properly?

THE GOOD, THE BAD AND THE UGLY

In the late 1970s, Paper Mate, a division of Gillette, introduced to the US market a revolutionary erasable ballpoint pen. They called it Erasermate, a brand name which typifies much of American branding – it is memorable, strong, gets straight to the point and has a positive link with an established house brand. It was highly successful in its home market and proved an interesting product for Europe. Unfortunately, though the name Erasermate was perfectly acceptable in certain European countries, in others it was unattractive. We undertook a name creation exercise for the whole of Europe and developed the name Replay. The name is strong, distinctive and protectable through Europe, alludes to the function of the product and is widely understood across Europe – in TV coverage of sports events the word is widely used and understood, even in non-English speaking countries. Replay is a good brand name. It is neither so completely abstract as to require enormous investment before it acquires significance, nor so descriptive as to be unprotectable or particularised to one country.

In contrast, many of us have heard rumours of such wonderful products as Sic and Pschitt (both French soft drinks), Creap (Japanese coffee creamer), Green Pile (Japanese lawn dressing), Super Piss (a Finnish product for unfreezing car locks) and Bum (Spanish potato crisps). Indeed, encountering such exotic brands is one of the more obscure pleasures of international travel. Most problem brands, however, have less obvious flaws; it may even be unfair to describe these brands as having flaws when the owners probably had no intention of marketing them outside their home markets and are not concerned that their brand occasions mirth among visiting foreigners. Rather, it is the more insidious problems which can really cause difficulties – brand names which are so descriptive they are not protectable, names with so little distinctiveness they are readily copied, or names which are so particular to one positioning that they lock the brand into that positioning without any chance of further development.

THE BRAND NAME SPECTRUM

The brand name Kodak is a pure invention. It is a collection of letters which is short, memorable, strong, both graphically and visually and yet has no 'core' of meaning whatsoever. It was adopted by a brave marketing man and, over decades, has developed into one of the most potent brand names in the world.

Sunsilk is an attractive name for shampoo. It has connotations of softness and associations with the great outdoors. It is by no means a pure invention but, rather, draws its strength from images and associations relevant to us all.

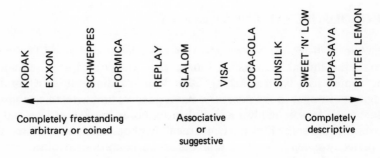

FIGURE 8.2   *The brand name 'spectrum'*

Bitter Lemon is purely descriptive of a lemon-based mixer drink. It has very little invention and hence is unprotectable.

These three brand names span the BRAND NAME SPECTRUM from totally free-standing names to completely descriptive names. (Figure 8.2). All brand names fall somewhere along this spectrum. Schweppes, a name with delightful in-built onomatopaeia, conveys images of effervescence. Formica is mainly an invented name but has a core of meaning. Visa is a name with associations of travel and crossing boundaries and Sweet 'n' Low is a name with a high descriptive content.

In general, the more descriptive a name the more it communicates immediately to the consumer. Unfortunately such names tend to be less distinctive and less protectable. In contrast, the more free-standing a name the less it immediately conveys to the consumer and the more the brand owner needs to invest in it to confer upon it the qualities of excellence and superiority he requires. Between these two extremes lie 'associative' names, those which are distinctive and protectable and yet communicate some appropriate message or messages to the consumer, perhaps subconsciously.

Companies tend, when developing new brand names, to seek descriptive names. It is somehow felt that such names will help sales and scant attention is paid sometimes to the longer-term implications. But why does the name need to contain an overt message? After all, the advertising, the graphics and the packaging all convey messages to consumers. So why use the brand name too to describe your product? To hazard the long-term success of the brand by adopting a descriptive name which is unprotectable is clearly absurd. But this is done constantly.

The answer is not necessarily to adopt totally invented names of the Kodak, Exxon or Xerox type and, indeed, few organisations have a sufficiently innovative product or a sufficiently large promotional budget to allow 'blue sky' branding of this type. But the middle route, the associative route, can and does result in powerful, attractive and protectable brand names. Kodak might have fared as well had Mr Eastman adopted a name such as Vista but would hardly have been in as powerful a market position today if he had called his company Super-Pic or Easi-Foto.

CONCLUSIONS

As segments become narrower and more specialised, and as national habits, tastes and markets become more sophisticated and more international, the job of the brand name becomes more critical. Companies and their brand or new product management must become increasingly aware of both the commercial and legal realities of trademarks.

Trademarks are under-recognised assets and under-utilised marketing and strategic weapons. A greater awareness of their potential importance, and a greater willingness to spend time and money in their development, application and protection will pay enormous dividends to those companies engaged in the daily battle for the consumer's attention.

9 Creative Execution

MERVYN KURLANSKY

THE DESIGNER'S RÔLE

Detailed knowledge of a brand's development and pure creativity both play distinct yet interrelated roles in the designer's formulation of the brand's image. Knowledge is essential in understanding the multiplicity of factors that affect the brand's success and allows for the proper analysis that leads to the appropriate creative constraints. Creativity is naturally required to imbue the brand with a unique image which is appropriate and appealing.

Creativity without analysis is often wasted effort. If the designer is locked away in an ivory tower and approached diffidently with a brief to come up with an image for a fully developed new product, the chances are that the results will not be appropriate. The client may be lucky. But why leave it to luck? The designer in his (or her) ivory tower is not a useful contributor to a sane, professional approach to brand development because the opportunity for analysis before the creative process starts is severely limited. The designer who applies experience and know-how in the analysis of proper information about the product will undoubtedly stand a better chance of coming up with the most appropriate solution.

The curious thing is that so many people do not think of design as a 'rational' exercise. Of course designers trade on those bits of magic that make good design great. But those bits of magic are only a very small part of a designer's capability and worth. So let us proceed on the premise that design is for the most part a rational and analytical exercise, contributing to a brand's development in many different ways.

The designer's rôle in the development of a brand is determined by the nature of the project but can start earlier than most brand owners think. There is little doubt that designers can contribute to a brand's image before any visual treatment emerges. Design considerations should be taken into account in developing a product's function, action, aesthetics, ergonomics, message and name. The emphasis of this chapter is on the rôle of graphic design in the development of a brand's image. But just as an interior designer contributes to the architect's task in designing a building, so can a graphic designer make a real contribution to the choice of a brand's name, as well as to determining its size and shape and the choice and nature of the packaging.

So the designer should be introduced into the development process at an early stage. The evolution of a brand is influenced by a number of disciplines. First, the marketing people, with the aid of researchers, determine the market opportunity that generates the new brand. That opportunity is analysed and the technical requirements of the product are defined. The technical development itself may show up new opportunities for the brand's formulation – this may change or improve the original definition. Such development can lead to a test or prototype product for internal appraisal. The market's response to this first effort may also be sought. Development continues until the product itself is right.

If during all this process the designer's expertise is on hand, not only does the designer become thoroughly familiar with the new brand's strengths and characteristics, but his experience is also available to advise on name, style, packaging, colours, typography, symbols – at the right point in the development process. Any development team is a mixture of disciplines. The disciplines contribute specific expertise in their own fields when the development requires it. But the whole development is enhanced further when a laboratory technician can influence the designer with his own ideas, or when the designer can influence the market researcher with his.

The designer is equipped to carry out the creative function by all the information which is received as a member of the development team. This information must be analysed. The main area of analysis is, of course, the market and this ultimately conditions the brand's identity and thus its design. The identity of a new brand has to be related to others competing in the same market – either as a recognisable part of a genre, or as a radical departure. Both approaches are appropriate and depend on the nature of the product. Any design must be distinctive, but it may be that it should respect the conventions established in its market in order to reassure purchasers.

Thus, for example, a Mars bar is recognisable as a chocolate bar by its shape, type of wrapping, its easy, short name and the use of large lettering. All these follow established mass-confectionery conventions. Alpen breakfast cereal also follows the 'muesli' conventions in terms of its box shape and the pictures of its ingredients. But it breaks away from a conventional approach by its use of colour: the box is black.

Other factors in the designer's analysis include the life expectancy of the brand – changes in the image of a brand now take place more frequently in order to retain market interest. Cadbury's Fruit and Nut chocolate bars and Heinz Baked Beans retain their distinctive image, although there is continual evolution in the detail of the package design.

If the new brand is aimed at both existing purchasers in a market sector, as well as attracting new purchasers to the sector and enlarging it, then a brand identity has to reassure and excite at the same time. When a new identity is required for an old product, decisions have to be made on available information as to whether to discard the old identity entirely or take an evolutionary approach respecting some of the old identity's familiarity.

THE BRAND NAME

It is not easy for a designer to work with a brand name that does not lend itself to the right design solution. If the analysis has led the designer to the conclusion that a short name would work best, and he has been handed a long name as a *fait accompli* – then there is a conflict. But the name's length is not the only consideration. The name itself conjures up images, feelings and colours that the designer must respect. The actual letters that make up the name can also present an opportunity or a restriction in the design solution.

There are different relationships between the brand's name and its visual identity. For instance, the identity may be a literal interpretation of the brand's name as is the case with Lion Brand stationery (Plate 9.1). Alternatively the identity may be based on the nature of the product as in Lyons Coffee (Plate 9.2). Or the name and the identity may be created together as a unified concept.

In this last category we once created the Tactics range of up-market men's toiletries (Plate 9.3). The name, the design of the bottles and the packaging were all conceived as a whole based upon detailed research and analysis of the market provided by the client in Japan. Although in this instance the designer did not develop the brand name, this does not mean it is never his job. Often better branding results are achieved if the designer is allowed a fuller rôle in developing the name and design as a total concept. But however the name is conceived, and whatever it is, the aim is to foster a unity between the name and the visual identity. This may develop over time but ultimately the name and the visual identity should each call the other to mind spontaneously.

THE FAMILY CIRCLE

A brand's identity rarely exists in isolation – except in the case of a one-product company. Surrounding the brand identity is the corporate identity of the manufacturer and there may also be various range identities. The corporate identity can play an important part in the brand's identity particularly when the manufacturer's reputation is high. For instance, in the case of real ale brands, the name of a long-established, locally based, dependable brewer is usually given a high profile in the overall identity of a brand.

Some companies have corporate and brand identities that are to all intents and purposes the same. Lucas Industries, for instance, has a strong corporate identity, which is also used on its products (Plate 9.4a,b). The identity is apparent on Girling brakes in the same way as on Lucas batteries – the variations between them are expressed only through the use of different colours. Other companies develop separate brand identities from the corporate identity, but use the corporate mark to support the brand. A good example of this approach is the Dulux paint brand logo which is juxtaposed with the ICI symbol on packaging and advertising (Plate 9.5). At the other end of the scale there are those companies that keep a very low profile with respect to their brands; for instance, the 'presence' of Procter & Gamble on its products is practically non-existent.

Hierarchies are also important. Consider this sequence: Cadbury-Schweppes, Cadbury, Cadbury's chocolate, Fruit and Nut. The reputation of each element, from the overall holding company to the actual brand, depends on and is affected by all the other elements. What emphasis is placed on which element depends on the particular case.

SERVICES AND PRODUCTS

From airline operators to book publishers, there is a tendency for service companies to involve their corporate identities closely in their branding. An obvious example is British Telecom whose corporate design pervades practically all its services and products. This giant company has an overwhelming image, especially since it was privatised. Nevertheless, it has services which take quite a different branding approach. Cellnet, the BT cellular telephone system, is a case in point.

The branding of manufactured products, such as consumer and industrial goods, is a composite process which involves the product designer's styling skills, the function and action of the product itself (Plate 9.6), its size, shape and form and the marketing and sales proposition that is formulated for it. The graphic designer is involved mainly in the labelling of the product and sometimes in the choice of colour. The packaging of the product should always reflect the overall selling proposition together with the advertising and promotional strategy and should never be designed in isolation.

Where the brand identity and the packaging are, in a sense, one and the same thing – i.e. when you remove the packaging you cannot tell the product from the competition, such as with coffee, soap powder, toothpaste, petrol, whisky – the identity is, in effect, the package design. The packaging has two main elements: the material and the mechanics of the package itself, and the graphics. The packaging must persuade and it must also be 'true' to the product. If the package holds out promises for the product that are not delivered it is a sure recipe for one purchase and no more. The product may determine the material of the packaging, which in turn determines the design. For instance, waxy milk cartons require screen printing and this limits the designer on the choice and intricacy of colour and form. (The waxy carton itself, incidentally, becomes part of the product's identity.)

Point of sale is also a consideration. The competition for attention of a crowded supermarket shelf may demand a particular level of impact with colour and lettering. Imagery can be used to exploit the effect of many packages of the same brand on the shelf. But once out of the shop, the package must go on working for the product and the brand image.

Statutory considerations are also increasingly important and have to be incorporated harmoniously, not simply added on. The UPC bars, the ingredients, the 'sell by' date, the guarantee – all should be 'designed in'. Analysis should also have determined what laws – copyright, safety, trades description – should be considered before design starts. Foreign language requirements should also be accommodated early on.

CONCEPT DEVELOPMENT

The first stage of the actual design process is the creation of the concept. The designer seeks to create an indentity which is unique, appropriate to the product or range and appealing to the identified market. Concepts vary enormously in the thinking and style that create them. The design may be purely decorative using colour, line and typography. But the best concepts also involve an original idea or juxtaposition of ideas. By matching analysis with creativity the designer's concept takes full account of his knowledge of the product – what is its value, its use, who is it for and what makes it unique. Originality of concept may be achieved using familiar images – visual clichés – in a novel way. Using familiar images can evoke a kind of nostalgia which gives a new product an instant 'past' or 'history' in the view of the market. The design concept has, however, to be appealing – a sense of pleasure which may come from images of luxury, or tradition or novelty or even fad. The pleasure may also come from the wit of the identity, for instance, when name and image interplay cleverly.

Most design concepts go through the fire of testing. Not only do the other disciplines in the development have their say, but even the Chairman's secretary may get involved. (Do not underestimate her power and influence!) Perhaps most importantly, the researchers will test the concept in the market to assess reaction where it counts. What happens from here is a gradual evolution of the original design concept. Fine tuning of colour, typography and form in relation to each other within the concept achieve the desired enhancement and the exact matching to market expectation. Changes can be demanded by new factors in the market place thrown up in the concept research, new developments in the product due to testing, and, of course, by ideas from other disciplines in the development team.

The painstaking work of design development is crucial to the creation of a successful brand image. One slip, however good the concept, can have a damaging effect on sales. From concept to the end of the development process, the designer needs a keen sense of opportunity. Within the terms of his analysis there are still many opportunities for accidental discoveries and 'creative leaps'. A surprising outcome must never be discounted.

PRODUCTION

The developed concept is now ready for production. Here there are many new influences on the outcome. For instance, in the Dulux Brilliant White paint concept, the original idea was for the whiteness of the paint to be expressed in blind embossed lettering. Actual embossing proved too expensive, however, so the eventual solution was an interpretation of the original idea.

At the production stage there are a host of similar considerations for the designer to take account of. Storage and shipping requirements may determine the shape, size and material of packaging. Certain printing processes are more cost effective on one material than another or more appropriate to large production runs. Safety standards must also be complied with. On bottle labelling the whole brand identity may be affected by the shape of the bottle, this having a direct influence on the shape and size of the label. Thus again it is important that the designer does not live in an ivory tower. He has to work with a project from the concept stage through to final production and interpret the needs of the consumer, the purchaser, the printer, the plant in a way which is cost-effective, appropriate and appealing to consumers.

CONCLUSIONS

There is no room in the development process for the isolated designer. Whatever a particular designer's ability, the best work will come from a thorough involvement in the development of the brand, proper analysis of the resulting information and a creative execution which takes all this into account – and which adds a spark of originality. Then the brand will have an image which is unique, appealing and appropriate. And with that Will o' the Wisp of true originality which surprises even its creator, the designer, and which defies both planning and the systematic approach, the brand will also have that bit of magic that makes it outstanding. But there is no accounting for bits of magic. Or Will o' the Wisps.

10 The Opportunity for World Brands

STEVE WINRAM

THE LONGEVITY OF THE BRAND

Tables 10.1 and 10.2 demonstrate a truly remarkable fact. They show that brands – those complex mixtures of product and consumer appeal – are not only capable of surviving for extraordinarily long periods, but that they have also been capable of maintaining their market position throughout sixty years of competition and development. We shall be examining the forces and strategies that lie behind the successes of these brands and the way in which these strategies must evolve in the future to deal with the marketing developments of the next decade.

To see why the extended life of brands is a surprising phenomenon, the production and marketing of branded products must be placed in a 'market' context. Manufacturing industry in advanced countries is, in general,

TABLE 10.1   *UK brand leaders*

1933	Current position
Hovis, bread	No. 1
Stork, margarine	No. 1
Kellogg's, cornflakes	No. 1
Cadbury's chocolate	No. 1
Rowntree, pastilles	No. 1
Schweppes, mixers	No. 1
Brooke Bond, tea	No. 1
Colgate, toothpaste	No. 1
Johnson's, floor polish	No. 1
Kodak, film	No. 1
Ever Ready, batteries	No. 1
Gillette, razors	No. 1
Hoover, vacuum cleaners	No. 1

SOURCE   Based on 1933 advertising expenditure, and current market surveys.

TABLE 10.2 *US brand leaders*

1923	Current position
Swift Premium, bacon	No. 1
Eastman Kodak, cameras	No. 1
Del Monte, canned fruit	No. 1
Wrigley, chewing gum	No. 1
Nabisco, biscuits	No. 1
Ever Ready, batteries	No. 1
Gold Medal, flour	No. 1
Gillette, razors	No. 1
Coca-Cola, soft drinks	No. 1
Campbell's, soup	No. 1
Ivory, soap	No. 1
Lipton, tea	No. 1
Goodyear, tyres	No. 1

SOURCE   Adapted from *Advertising Age*, 19 September 1983.

composed of large organisational units that compete with each other through means other than the pricing of their output.

Typically, competition takes the form of continuous product innovation and advertising. But these forms of competition set up their own dynamic which in turn poses further strategic problems for the producer. During periods of rapid technological advance, these trends are exacerbated. As information transfer on an intra-country and inter-country basis becomes more highly developed, often as a result of manufacturer competition, the process of competition through product differentiation becomes more difficult. Two of the processes that stand in the way of the longevity of brands are the product cycle and the life-cycle of the brand.

The Product Cycle

One of the great pressures on manufacturers is the product cycle – the process by which advanced products become standardised. Manufacturers can no longer comfortably rely upon product supremacy in a world where technological developments quickly stimulate not only consumer demand but also an imitative process amongst competitive manufacturers.

Products that once led the world as triumphs of innovation, such as the mass-produced car, the personal calculator and Hi Fi equipment, are eventually copied and reproduced the world over. Competition through the introduction of new technology into production processes suffers the same fate. The introduction by Ford of the car production line in the USA was soon copied abroad. The new robotic functions in car manufacture are likely to succumb to the same fate – they are concurrently being introduced in the UK,

US, Italy, Germany and Japan. Today the car is the symbol of the high technology product that has become a standardised commodity. The ever-shortening time-lag between innovation and imitation mean that products can quickly and efficiently be produced by competitors at home or abroad and in less advanced countries.

As products become standardised, they effectively become 'price constrained', their commodity status gives rise to low brand loyalty, and in the face of tough competition, manufacturers become loath to trade on price differentials for fear of cutting demand too savagely if they price too high or inducing a price war if they price too low.

Clearly, in a situation where technology is rapidly diffused, product quality is largely uniform, and prices are constrained, production tends to move to those countries that have a natural cost advantage. Thus cars are produced in Brazil, electronic equipment in Taiwan, television sets and heavy construction equipment in South Korea, and personal calculators and microcomputers in Malaysia. These trends in the location of new centres of production – the rapid rise of the newly industrialised countries of the Far East and Latin America – can be traced to precisely these competitive pressures.

Against this background, individual products or brands are perceived as having a short rather than an indefinite life expectancy.

The Life-cycle of the Brand

Built into much manufacturing/marketing philosophy is the notion that brands have a 'life-cycle'. Brands are developed in response to a perceived consumer need, a gap in the market left by other producers. They are enthusiastically developed, promoted in a new way, gain market share and struggle to stave off competition. As the new product gains acceptance, as its market share stabilises, it becomes a predominant feature of the market. But as the product ages, as the support for its qualities wanes, as the market itself declines, some manufacturers are prepared to let their products run down – milk them as 'cash cows' before they fade from the market place altogether.

What is the basis of survival for the manufacturer who lives in this sort of world? There are three broad fronts on which the manufacturer can act:

(1) He can try to escape the profit-crushing constraints of a commodity market through innovation, through the constant development and improvement of an old product.
(2) He can try to evolve totally new products, which operate in a new makret, and which afford the possibility of new profits.
(3) He can attack the cost base which defines his profit margins, by trying to gain economies of scale.

Clearly, manufacturers will aim to use all of these strategies, the mix of which will depend upon the stage in the product cycle that each manufacturer (or the industry in which it operates) has reached.

Very few manufacturers operate at the forefront of technology in a product sense, even though their production processes may be highly advanced. They operate in markets which are more nearly 'commodity' or highly standardised markets than highly 'product differentiated' markets, and hence are more prone to incursion from other production centres around the world that have cheaper relative (labour) costs.

The pressures of product market convergence have been reinforced in the 1970s by two further developments. On one hand, the inflation prevalent throughout the world during this period put pressure on corporate profits as manufacturers were unable to respond to rising costs of production. On the other hand, consumer market growth itself has begun to diminish as the Second World War baby boom has matured and population growth in the major markets of the world has slowed down, producing static markets. For these reasons corporate priorities have switched – many manufacturers now aim to become the 'low-cost' producer in their product category.

Recommendations in terms of advertising and marketing strategy for the 1980s turn on a parallel trend of convergence in consumer markets. The technological advances (especially in television satellite and cable communications) that result from the dynamic of industrial competition are inducing a convergence in habit, life-style and culture amongst consumer market segments across the world. The successful marketers of the 1980s will be those that treat these market segments as global, not local, markets. It will be the economies of scale that result from this switch in emphasis that will distinguish the 'low cost producer' from the rest: the manufacturer who can incorporate superior quality at constant values into his products from those struggling for survival in an increasingly competitive world.

Some companies believe they can create a refuge from competitors by burrowing into one market. However, this kind of niche in the context of global competition becomes analogous to a pothole. When a strong competitor targets a market section that includes that niche, it will have the effect of a steamroller paving over the entire sector.

Arthur D. Little, Inc., Management Consultants

Commitment to this strategy involves being sharp in the definition of long-term objectives, frank about strengths and weaknesses, clear about the company's position in a world market, and sure of the enduring quality of its products. And, most of all, it means a commitment to making progress in the market place on the only truly long-term basis – product superiority.

Superior Product Quality

Superior product quality is the basis of any brand character, which is the mix of rational and emotional factors that make up the product's relationship with the consumer. It is this relationship that lies at the heart of the creation of brands. Serious marketers know that building a strong brand character means a fuller relationship with the consumer and a better position for the brand. They also know that the longevity of their brand is helped by good marketing, but it is founded on superior product performance, which is founded on the effectiveness of their technological organisation.

This is why serious marketers have been determined to invest in technology – never considered as providing much leverage, for example, in the food business before – to provide the means to achieve that happiest of all situations: lower costs, fewer price increases and higher quality.

OBSTACLES TO BRAND BUILDING

The establishment of a strong and enduring brand character is being made more difficult by all of these factors:

(1) Depressed or static economies are creating increased competition for market share.
(2) Product quality is converging, increasing technological parity among major marketers.
(3) Governmental restrictions on brand marketing continue, including regulation of advertising copy and media.
(4) The influence of the retailer is growing in many parts of the world, diverting marketing funds to the retailer.
(5) Pressure is continuing from low-price or generic brands in many basic packaged good categories.
(6) Marketing expenses are growing, as manufacturers respond to the escalating cost of reaching the consumer.

Under these pressures, some packaged goods manufacturers have been nudged towards cutting product costs, curtailing research and development investment and reducing advertising expenditures. They have edged away from three key elements on which brand character is built: product quality, product differentiation and communication to the consumer.

THE OPPORTUNITY FOR WORLD BRANDS

One of the striking aspects of the problems facing manufacturers is that they exist throughout the developed world. As the problems for marketers are similar in different countries, might they also present similar opportunities? Are social developments making outmoded the old idea that the differences between nations with regard to this or that durable, cosmetic or coffee were crucial for marketing strategy?

Consumer convergence in demography, habits and culture are increasingly leading manufacturers to a consumer-driven rather than a geography-driven view of their marketing territory. The most advanced manufacturers are recognising that there are probably more social differences betwen midtown Manhattan and the Bronx, two sectors of the same city, than between midtown Manhattan and the 7th Arrondissement of Paris. This means that when a manufacturer contemplates expansion of his business, consumer similarities in demography and habits rather than geographic proximity will increasingly affect his decisions.

Marketers will be less likely to tailor products to the differing national wants and more likely to operate on the basis of the common needs for their products.

World Demographic Convergence

Trends of vast significance to consumer marketing, such as the decline of the nuclear family, the changing rôle of women as evidenced by increasing female employment, static ageing populations and higher living standards, are common to large segments of the modern industrial world. These convergences of demography, behaviour and shared cultural elements are creating a more favourable climate for acceptance of a single product and positioning across a wide range of geography.

World cultural convergence

At the same time as demography is converging, television and motion pictures are creating elements of shared culture. This cultural convergence is facilitating the establishment of multinational brand characters. The worldwide proliferation of the Marlboro brand would not have been possible without TV and motion picture education about the virile rugged character of the American West and the American cowboy, helped by increasing colour TV penetration in all countries. At the same time, TV programmes such as 'Dallas' and films such as 'Star Wars' and 'E.T.' have crossed many national boundaries to achieve world awareness for their plots, characters, etc.

Observers believe that cultural convergence will proceed at an accelerated rate through the next decade, particularly with the deployment of L-SAT high-power TV satellites and increased cable penetration. The European Space Agency (ESA) launched its first satellite, the Orbital Test Satellite

(OTS), in 1978. The OTS has already completed many tests such as the 'Eurikon' experiment in which the European Broadcasting Union broadcast an international selection of television programmes that were simultaneously translated both into teletext and the spoken word. Satellite TV, a UK company, has introduced the first commercial European satellite network, and currently broadcasts nightly to Finland, Norway, Switzerland and Malta.

The British Government has also announced its decision to back the L-SAT programme by investing £77 million in a British satellite craft. France, Germany, Italy, Luxembourg, Switzerland and the Nordic countries expect to have their own five-channel satellites transmitting by 1987. Needless to say there will be a high degree of overspill of transmissions from the new 'super stations' of these European countries.

The appeal of foreign-language programmes whose satellite 'footprint' passes over the boundaries of other nations will be increased by the advent of multiple audio-channels to accompany each video channel, making it possible to provide a choice of languages on any satellite channel. Britons will then be able to enjoy a French soap opera, or a Germany documentary, alongside their more regular fare.

These developments will reduce cultural barriers as countries exchange their media output through satellite networks, for the first time allowing viewers free access to international television without the barrier of language.

Media Convergence

Cable too is a worldwide phenomenon. Substantial proportions of the US and Europe are already wired for the reception of multichannel cable networks. The US leads the way in this, as in many other areas of communication technology, but throughout Europe plans are well developed for the sort of cable expansion that will equip each country for the needs of the rest of the century. In Japan, a successful 'wired city' experiment at Hi Ovis has shown the viability of fully interactive cable-based technology that provide not only entertainment but a complete communication service between school, offices and homes. The US currently has 30 million cable-receiving households compared with only 3 million five years ago, and over half the 90 million American households will be linked to cable in the next ten years.

Cable has already begun to erode the US networks' share of the national television audience, down from 93 to 90 per cent. As more cable stations start to carry advertising (70 per cent of systems do already) they will eat into the network share of advertising revenue as well.

Internationally, much of cable's promise as an advertising medium stems from its ability to attract audiences through selective programming aimed at more clearly defined groups than the mass audiences of the major networks. Multinational advertisers with a specific target audience in each country will be able to reach their target segment through a cable channel concentrating on their specific interest.

The Economics of World Brands

Market leaders' priorities are now focusing on a common objective which was not among their priorities in previous decades: to work diligently to be the low-cost producer in their market. Thus 'Kellogg is totally dedicated to being and staying a low-cost producer of ready-to-eat cereals around the world'. The company says it will apply new technology 'to produce, distribute, and market our products with greater efficiency'.

Such companies are moving through the various stages in the life of a multinational corporation. And as they pass from the stage at which they co-ordinate marketing and production in different countries to the stage at which they centralise production, distribution and marketing by continent, the need for pan-regional and world marketing is emerging as the heart of their business strategy. Continued cost inflation and the competitive intensity of maturing packaged goods markets has also brought to the fore the economic logic of world brands – the opportunity for international economies of scale as the basis of long-term strategic security.

Low costs are the priority as a sound base for all the other steps needed to build growth. The most thoughtful companies are therefore adopting a new approach to international marketing. After the vicissitudes of the 1950s and 1960s, more companies are now reaching the status of having acquired 'critical mass' in various regions of the world. They are now starting to turn from primary concern about 'return on acquisition investment' and 'overhead recovery' towards getting to grips with long-term franchise building across each world region.

The progressive harmonisation of headquarters and local management culture and style, evolving from more frequent two-way movement of personnel, is enhancing the likelihood of successful adoption and execution of global business strategies. In Europe, management's strategic thinking is beginning to broaden to match the dimensions of the Common Market as legislative harmonisation focuses attention on pan-European issues.

Companies have passed through the age when most of them treated the 'Overseas Division' as the poor cousin of the organisation, struggling to compete in foreign markets with strongly established indigenous competitors. The international divisions of many companies are now beginning to 'come of age' and receive their rightful allocation of corporate resource, if only for the practical reason that corporate earnings growth in many multinationals is today often provided by non-domestic markets.

The strategic value of pan-regional branding lies in the economies of scale it may afford across the company's business system, to help make the company the low-cost producer. Where the economies lie will vary by product category, across research and development, materials purchasing, manufacturing, distribution and advertising. The optimum business system for a European beer, for example, is markedly different from that for chewing gum, but the principle is the same. Secure franchise-protected volumes at the regional scale can allow a company to build a price/cost/value structure which will eventually put it out of reach of competition.

HOW TO MANAGE A WORLD BRAND

In the past, the successes in world branding have been few and have been achieved by virtue of the sheer will and far-sighted commitment of managements who stayed consistently with a long-term vision for the business. Procter & Gamble is a company in this category that comes to mind.

Consider, for example, the Pampers brand. It was introduced in the United States in the late 1960s. Pampers created the disposable diaper market by providing a product that was more convenient and more absorbent than cloth diapers at a price consumers were willing to pay. Pampers is now Procter & Gamble's largest brand and is sold on a similar strategy almost all over the world. If the Pampers business was a separate company, it would rank in the top one-third of the 'Fortune 500' list.

What kind of practical action is required to achieve this size and momentum in world markets? First, it requires *structure*.

Some of the world's best marketers have formed new organisations, whilst others find themselves with extensive overseas operations which together lack overall perspective. Because structure and strategy are so closely interlinked, the beginning of worldwide co-ordination of activity lies in the attainment of a common corporate perspective.

Today, cultural differences between the operating arms of companies are sometimes more responsible than cultural differences between marketing areas in slowing the progress of pan-regional branding. The most advanced manufacturers realise that in today's marketing environment it is not the sum of individual or regional responsibilities which ensure a company's success, but an all encompassing corporate perspective. A new structure must therefore apply that overview to create well-developed systems for effective communication. The new structure will allow regional management to come together to examine the impact of their marketing effort and to assess it in the light of a regional or global point of view. Therefore, a prerequisite for the world brand winners is the ability to organise and communicate globally. The organisation and communication methods which served a company well within its home territory will not prove as successful when it expands its horizons. Most major marketing companies today are in a state of transition between country-localised and more broadly centralised forms of organisation.

When a company first looks beyond its home boundaries, it generally begins with an export operation; then opens marketing companies overseas with their own manufacturing plant; then begins to co-ordinate its own marketing and production across the range of countries with which it does business; and eventually centralises production, distribution and marketing by continent. During this process companies will have both a locally oriented and centrally oriented management of co-ordination system in force simultaneously. And this places a premium on an efficient system to harness the best creative minds in a region of the world – and give them the opportunity to develop brands for an entire region of the world, and not simply for one market – to find brands that can transcend national borders previously thought inviolate.

So that what emerges from the process is not the lowest common denominator but brands with the force to make themselves felt in widely differing parts of the world.

Thus the creative process becomes even more challenging and exciting – marketers in each location will be dependent on the intuitive judgement of locally based management, but this effort will be marshalled to a single-minded overall branding strategy.

There is then a real marketing learning curve that allows the progressive refinement of a success formula, as pan-regional brands broaden their experience country by country. Success in managing this system of multinational input against a common strategic objective will distinguish the world brand winners of the 1980s and 1990s – learning to ride the multinational learning curve, based on the progressive refinement of a successful formula, as pan-regional brands broaden their experience country by country.

Key Research Process

Without structure, there can be no strategy. But once a company abandons its country by country approach to selling the same product in favour of one which can capitalise upon the economies of co-ordited action, strategy becomes paramount. The basis of strategy is research, which is why the most advanced manufacturers are now seeking to monitor objectively the progress of their brands across the world. And why pilot research programmes are underway tracking brands within major packaged goods categories, using a broad-based sample. Follow-up studies are being conducted periodically and trend information derived.

The results of this research are allowing companies to assess the fundamental strength or weakness of a brand's character, and the specific aspects of its reputation which are contributing most of its overall status. This information is proving enormously useful from a predictive and diagnostic standpoint – helping to point the way to remedial action and to provide indications of the brand's future prospects.

Analysis of this research is allowing companies to derive a single figure 'Brand Character Index', much like a share-of-market number or Day-After-Recall score.

This is not a direct measure of 'advertising effectiveness'. It is simply a framework or structure which allows the marketer to assess decisively the extent to which any particular brand lives up to the company's chosen central positioning strategy for that brand. This information allows the apparently ephemeral subject of brand character to be managed by objectives in the same way as most other aspects of an efficient company's business.

Every brand requires a consistent strategic focus and a distinct reason for being. And every brand deserves a trial in an objective court against those criteria. The Brand Character Index enables a multinational company to measure the extent to which a brand's character differs across national boundaries, as well as the changes in its level in any one country over time. In simple terms, the key point of reference in the development of an international measure of 'brand character' is the clear definition of the desired character for the brand.

The intellectual process of defining objectives in this way is the critical first step. The process will then involve a two-way interaction – on the one hand, the actual position of the brand's character as revealed by market research; on the other, the marketer's detailed perception of where the brand's character should be, even if the product is currently not quite perceived in those terms by the consumer. The Brand Character Index measures the gap between the actual and the optimum brand character.

This technique is enabling the multinational advertiser to set measurable objectives for advertising and monitor progress towards those objectives – around the world, and over time – in a rational way.

Armed with this information, the most modern marketers are achieving a new perspective on world markets. From the high ground, they can survey the world battlefield for their brands, observe the deployment of their forces, and plan their marketing in a coherent way – to seize all the economies of scale available to them.

Countries, rather than regions within a country, will be the test markets of the future. Advertising executions will originate with one creative group and then, through the Darwinian process of market place success, grow into regional or global use.

All these factors set the conceptual framework within which a truly pan-regional brand can exist in the years ahead. The international need is the starting point. Research will be conducted to look for market similarities between countries, not to seek out differences. Similarities will be the new fuel for growth.

ADVERTISING FOR WORLD BRANDS

Why has advertising been blessed with continuous growth through the recent world recession? What service do advertising agencies provide that has endured the slings and arrows of outrageous commercial fortune?

Advertising agencies try to provide their clients with a unique service: with advertising that is neither tiresomely dull, nor brilliantly irrelevant; with an understanding of social psychology as well as economic geography; with the long-range vision to plan strategically, and the short-term market knowledge to promote tactically; with the calm insight of a social psychologist, and the aggressive instinct of a great salesman; with the ability to negotiate with media owners about airing commercials, and with movie stars about appearing in them; with the talent to write music as well as words, and to cast, direct and produce films; to inspire company sales forces to sell goods, and retailers to stock them; with involvement as well as objectivity, and passionate commitment as well as honest criticism; and with the wisdom and vision to fulfil for their clients the rôle of the constitutional monarch – 'to advise, to encourage, and to warn'.

Changes in demography increase the importance of expanding market share, upgrading consumers' preferences to premium products, and operating on a worldwide basis. Thus the advertising expertise required to introduce new products and world products, and to execute competitive as well as defensive marketing efforts for existing brands, continues to increase.

Knowledge has value; and its value is even greater during a period of turmoil and change in the business environment, when operations are more global than local. Nowhere is this likely to be more true than in the fast-moving world of communications and communications technology.

The world advertising market is growing, and within the overall growth the share held by multinational agencies is increasing, as large corporations strive for greater co-ordination and centralisation of their international marketing activities.

This chapter is based on an article first published in the International Journal of Advertising, *vol. 3, no. 1, 1984.*

11 Branding – the Retailer's Viewpoint

TERRY LEAHY

INTRODUCTION

I recently shared a lift with a senior sales executive of a major British food manufacturer. He had just emerged from my company's buying office with the news that one of his major brands, a household name, was being dropped. During the awkward silence that these short journeys seem to produce, his expression was an odd mixture of suppressed rage and a plea for understanding.

He was not the first to suffer the experience and is unlikely to be the last. In such circumstances it is possible to understand why the emergence of the major multiple retailer is seen by some as a Biblical plague intended for the Egyptians but visited upon the manufacturer of branded goods instead. Manufacturers recall the heady days of branding in the sixties when the 'Fab Four' were Product, Promotion, Price and Place rather than a group of musicians from Liverpool.

In their view, the retailer should have left the manufacturer to get on with the marketing, and the techniques of yesteryear would still be working well and Brands would still be king.

To view the retailer as solely responsible for the problems facing manufacturers' brands in recent years, is, of course, about as sensible as the captain of the *Titanic* accusing the iceberg of bad navigation! These are difficult times for the Brand Manager, however, and the retailer is posing many new challenges and threats. For a manager to steer his brand through the eighties and nineties he has to understand the changing patterns emerging in the total distribution process. He has to be aware of Retail Marketing Strategies and ensure they are aligned to his own. He has to understand the rôle of Store Brands and Generics in order to benefit from them, or at least co-exist with them. He has to accept the paradox that in an age when consumers want more choice and more products, more brands will fail than ever before.

116

RETAILING STRATEGIES

Retailing is practised in every country in the world. However, the extent of its development varies a great deal from country to country. Since manufacturers' brands are not yet particularly troubled by the concentrated buying power of Eskimo trading posts, or by aggressive discounting among the tribal barter systems of New Guinea, I will concentrate mainly on the United Kingdom. If we look at the retail scene there today, what trends are apparent and what factors underlie these?

First, we must take note of the declining proportion of consumer expenditure accounted for by the retail sector, down from 57.2 per cent in 1972 to 50.9 per cent in 1982. The retailer clearly has his own survival battle to conduct and must adapt to be successful.

Secondly, the industry remains tremendously competitive. The efficient survive, and our record in producing new economies of scale and in introducing new technologies has been second to none among major industries. The intense competition in the food sector during the last decade has been marked by rapid integration. This trend will be repeated in other retail sectors as specialist multiples emerge with proven retail formats.

Thirdly, the emergence of the major multiple is really a sign of the retail industry reaching maturity. The professional management skills developed in the areas of manufacturing, finance, purchasing and marketing have found fertile ground in retailing, consolidating and building upon the achievements of the great retailing pioneers.

Fourthly, retail formats are now much more similar than they are different. In each major sector a way of trading has developed which has become a benchmark, producing similar range, price and promotional policies and incurring similar cost structures. As a result the retailer is now adopting the techniques of branding to differentiate himself in the eyes of the consumer.

Finally, the capacity for innovation would appear to be inexhaustible. Committed investment from established companies has competitors leap-frogging each other with new and, usually, improved standards. The very last word in retailing opens about once a week on average! There is still plenty of room, however, for the entrepreneur with a string of retail companies from drugs to frozen foods, making spectacular stock market debuts in recent years.

THE EMERGENCE OF MULTIPLE OR MASS RETAILERS

The evolution of retailing during the past twenty-five years from the fragmented, small-scale, 'Mum and Dad' era to today's supermarket, superstore and warehouse chains has changed the face of retailing.

No longer can each branch manager run his store individually, in isolation from the demands, requirements and advantages of the chain. Research has shown that such things as location, size relative to population within a given area, store layout and placement, inventory levels and stocking can be both quantified and qualified, and that this knowledge can be applied on a national basis.

These factors have, in turn, led to a need on the part of retailers to develop as an entity, as a distinctive 'brand' representing standards of quality, cleanliness, layout, choice and availability no matter where the store is located.

Just as with hotel chains, fast food restaurants and car rental companies, multiple retailers have developed predictable and powerful brands – the stores themselves.

The contrast with brand marketing is obvious. Had the second Mars bar ever sold tasted entirely different from the first, it is unlikely that Mars would have become a household name. Until the retailer recognised that he must have one common goal – the goal of the best shopping service for his customer – then he could never hope to develop a lasting franchise. Today's retailer has centralised his control. Policy is created in the centre and is executed through the branches.

This may be finely tuned over the coming decades as scanning information allows us to be more sensitive to local buying profiles, but the levers will still be pulled from the centre. Stores cost money, a lot of money, and nothing the customer experiences on a shopping trip today happens by accident. Everything from the location of the store down to the placement of the price tickets is designed to be an integral part of the retail product.

Once manufacturers begin to think of us as product managers just like they are, understanding us will not be so hard. Like manufacturers, we are in business to satisfy our customers' needs better than anyone else, and develop a lasting competitive advantage in doing so. For the retailer this is a three-stage process:

(1) He must understand the customer profiles that exist in the marketplace.
(2) He must determine his response by deciding exactly what his business is and to whom it is targetted.
(3) He must position himself with his customer so that he is perceived to meet his needs better than anyone else.

For this process to be successful it must be based upon a meaningful differentiation of products, services and cost structures.

Major chain store operations function in many hundreds of different markets. Each store is in a different market place, each product group constitutes a different market. Each market, moreover, is not composed of identical consumers. It is only by understanding and reacting to the particular requirements of each specific group of customers in each market, that we can successfully position ourselves. In Tesco, for example, that task involves 20 000 products, 400 stores and 8 million customer transactions per week.

THE RÔLE OF STORE BRANDS

Resist, for one moment, the image of a retailer as a fanatic waging a holy war on all manufacturers' brands in general, and yours in particular, and think instead of someone just like you trying to give the customer satisfaction, profitably. It is apparent that the retailer must never become dogmatic about own-label. The needs of the customer come first, and within this hierarchy of priorities own-label or the store brand is a means to an end, never an end in itself. It should be in response to a market opportunity, it should not be imposed upon consumers because we have decided it is good for our business.

The reason store brands are on the increase is because the climate today is right in terms of the consumer, the retailer, and the manufacturer. Tomorrow may be a different story.

THE CONSUMER

Today's consumers are liberated. They can shop where they want, when they want. They have more choice in how to spend their time and their money, and shopping is expected to fit into the consumer's timetable, not the other way round. More and more shopping, particularly food shopping, is unplanned.

This means that consumers want and are able to enjoy more flexibility, more convenience and more choice in their shopping and in the products they buy. They require modern stores with easy access, ample car parking and long opening hours. They want to shop in a pleasant clean environment with helpful efficient staff. They expect to find a wide range of products which will give the best possible combination of choice, quality and price.

Be in no doubt, the retailer who is sensitive to these changes, who commits investment, overcomes all the obstacles and builds the kind of store today's consumer wants, delivers a service which is of considerable and lasting benefit. It is my experience that the customer repays us with an enduring loyalty. The important point is that the loyalty is directed toward the store, the customer's store, and is stronger than for any individual product or service.

Within the context of a personal store the consumer is much less reliant upon the assurance of branding and is able to exercise individual discretion on price and quality. In such circumstances it should be no surprise that when a store offers a product under its own name of the same high quality as a brand, but at a lower price, the customer will buy that product.

THE RETAILER

Why is own-label important to the retailer? Recent years have seen intense competition and integration within the retail industry. The food multiple has emerged from this process stronger and leaner, but now finds that competition comes from other multiples with increasingly similar formats. As the consumer demands more from a store so the stakes increase and the retailer today must differentiate himself in order to guarantee a satisfactory return on investment. Store branding is seen as the solution.

For many years manufacturers have used the techniques of branding successfully. Branding can ensure that consumers develop a loyalty for a product regardless of outlet or competition, ideally to the point where the consumer buys the brand not the product. Retailers have now recognised that a supermarket need not be just a place to buy a selection of brands. Instead, the shop itself, its location, its atmosphere, the service it offers, the range of goods and prices, can become the brand and retailers can begin to extract the benefits which investment in branding can bring. The value which the store name acquires can be transferred to a range of goods which themselves reinforce the image of the store.

THE MANUFACTURER

The manufacturer has relied successfully on branding to ensure distribution of his products to the market. However, economic recession, retailer integration and market fragmentation lead to difficult conditions in which to operate branding. In the food sector branding, wrongly, became synonymous with marketing. Branding like own-label is a means to an end not an end in itself. It is a method which must be capable of adjustment as conditions alter. As belts tighten, manufacturers cut their investment in marketing and product development, which is the very seed corn of brand growth. This has led to the familiar downward spiral apparent in so many markets. An under-supported brand, unable to sustain the premium pricing which is its *raison d'être*, cuts price to sustain volume. This in turn forces another paring of costs thus further eroding the brand franchise.

This process has been taking place at precisely the time when the consumer is becoming more aware of alternatives and the retailer is offering better alternatives via store brands.

How then does own-label assist the retailer? The benefits may be grouped under six headings.

(1) Market Planning

The retailer needs to develop total markets for growth and profit, not just isolated products or brands. If we think of a market as being made up of products common to a purchasing decision then our job is to present the customer with the fullest choice, offering the best value for money. In a self-service environment it requires considerable market planning to communicate this choice clearly to the customer. If you do not believe me, stand in front of a badly merchandised toiletries display for a few moments, then close your eyes and see if you can remember what you have been offered.

Properly handled, own-label can be used to ensure co-ordinated range development by filling in gaps left by brands or by covering a market in its entirety. In the final analysis the main objective of the manufacturer's brand is the profitable growth of that brand and not the growth of the market. The requirement of each are not always compatible, and this can result in an imbalance of development.

(2) Control

Own-label is the property of the retailer and therefore under his absolute control. If we see a chance to develop a market in a particular direction we can use own-label to respond quickly and in the manner we want.

(3) Innovation

New product development which relies on branding to reach the market place often involves long lead times, heavy investment and high launch costs. The financial commitment for a manufacturer is sometimes so large that critical decisions about the nature of the product lean toward risk aversion. As a result we see too many 'me too' products rather than genuinely innovative products. The retailer does not have to buy distribution, launch costs are much lower and risks can be taken. In an increasing number of sectors, own-label is the shortest, cheapest and most successful new product development route for the retailer and the manufacturer.

(4) Choice

Own-label provides an alternative choice to the retailer and to the consumer. There can be little doubt that a number of important consumer product markets became stifled because of manufacturer monopoly or, more typically, oligopoly. The presence of the retailer's brand has brought new competition, provides an alternative in terms of range and price level, and has stimulated improvements in product choice and quality.

(5) Loyalty

I have already shown that the retailer must have an identity. Own-label brings the store right into the shopper's home. It is unique to that store and says things which cannot be copied by the competition. However, this cuts both ways. One bad own-label product can undermine an entire range of products, together with the overall store image.

(6) Cost

It takes a lot of investment to create a brand. We have already made that investment in our stores. Own-label products seldom require additional promotional investment and are therefore cheaper to develop. The customer pays less and the retailer can make a higher margin.

THE FUTURE OF BRANDED GOODS

The rise of the multiple retailer and the growth of own-label may suggest an unhealthy future for manufacturers' brands. When you are competing against an own-label for shelf space it must seem like playing a game where your opponent is also the rule-maker and the referee. Ultimately, I believe this will not be the case. A small minority of retailers are totally own-label, and this will continue. The majority will look to manufacturers' brands for profitable growth. The enormous reserves of market knowledge and product skills possessed by the manufacturer will continue to benefit the consumer and the retailer.

In my own sector, the food industry, a major review is already underway. Manufacturers are reassessing their brand strategies in the light of changed conditions. Retail concentration is here to stay, and is good for all. The modern retailer is efficient and invests heavily to meet the needs of the consumer. The modern store is the perfect 'shop window' for branded products. The challenge for the brand manager is to align his marketing strategy with that of the retailer. The retailer is no longer the salesman for the manufacturer, he is the buyer for the consumer. It is a subtle shift of position, but today it means that no brand is guaranteed distribution unless it meets the needs of the consumer and the retailer.

What brand strategies will be successful? There is probably no simple formula to guarantee the success of a brand. In my company we look at almost one thousand new products every year. No two products are alike, and the reasons for success or failure are not always consistent. One or more of the following features, however, are usually present when a product is a winner.

International Brands

The strength of the international brand is that it comes to the market-place as a proven success. It is much easier to persuade the retailer to support a product if there is hard evidence that it is going to succeed. International marketing can greatly extend the product life-cycle and can reduce the reliance on any one market, making it much easier to cope with the retail conditions which prevail.

High Tech. Brands

Superior product performance is the most enduring brand strength of all. It takes a good deal of wise investment to sustain a technological advantage and this tends to limit the brand portfolio.

But if you have built a quality into your brand which cannot be copied, then you are unique. Unless the customer buys your brand they do not get the benefit. The reason why own-label penetration is low in the confectionery, petfood and coffee markets is because there are brands present with product qualities the retailer cannot match.

Low Cost Brands as a Result of Manufacturing Efficiency

These are brands which consistently deliver quality at a price which others struggle to meet. Secondary brands cannot compete because they do not have the volume and it is difficult, for the same reason, for own brands to get a foothold. Their price stability can also give the customer a strong impression of value for money.

Marketing/Distribution Skills

These are not really inherent in the brand, but possessed by the organisation. The asset is people; marketing professionals who know their market-place, know the retail trade and know how to set the marketing mix.

High Growth Markets

Why pull against the tide when you can run with it with far less effort? Even in the worst economic conditions there are always growth markets. While it is true there is a high level of product failure, a properly managed brand in a growth market has a future.

Lifestyle Markets

These are products which respond to subtle shifts in consumer behaviour and which are in tune with consumers' aspirations. In the food sector today five life-style 'markets' enjoying real growth are Health, Freshness, Natural, Quality/Premium and Convenience.

Innovative Brands

The build-a-better-mousetrap strategy. Static markets can be transformed by products which look at an old problem in a fresh way.

Target Brands

There is a good deal of talk about segmentation of the mass market. Brands which identify an emerging consumer profile can create a very strong franchise albeit within a relatively confined market.

CONCLUSIONS

The future for branding is more exciting and challenging than ever before. Markets change and every new shift presents a threat for some and an opportunity for others. The retailer is now a powerful third force in the market place alongside the consumer and the manufacturer.

Clearly major opportunities exist today for retailers to develop own or store brands, primarily in segments which offer high volume or in segments where gaps have been left by the major manufacturers of branded goods. These developments will not only allow retailers to be more in control of their own destiny and business, but will also allow them to further cement the all-important relationship between themselves and their customers.

12 The Branding of Services

RUSSELL TAYLOR

THE GROWTH OF THE SERVICE SECTOR

As the more advanced or mature economies of the world evolve progressively towards higher standards of living, involving higher costs of living, higher levels of education, and the increased availability of advanced education for their populations, there is an increase in the availability of 'brain power', and a subsequent decrease in the supply of 'muscle power'. In short, our endless quest for progress and improvement leads, on both the individual and national level, to the steady conversion of brawn to brain. This steady conversion process causes a series of changes over time.

The most important of these is the gradual erosion of the manufacturing competitiveness of a nation. In recent years we have seen clear examples of this in the iron and steel industries of leading industrial nations, including Britain, the United States, Japan and West Germany. The same has happened too, to the same countries, in shipbuilding. We have seen also the increasing inability of the automotive industries of Western Europe and the USA to compete in mass markets, and the increasing ability of the Japanese and other Asian countries to dominate these segments. And even the Japanese motor industry is now undertaking manufacturing in Taiwan and eyeing nervously the growing strength of Korea. What we are witnessing is the price which a country pays as it increasingly moves from a secondary or manufacturing economy towards a tertiary or service-based economy.

The reason for this gradual yet inevitable shift is quite simply that as a nation develops an increasing supply of expensive brain power it becomes less and less able to compete in the area of, relatively speaking, inexpensive muscle power. Industries which rely heavily on muscle to be competitive consequently wither and die, and their place is taken by industries which require a higher percentage of more expensive brain power – namely service industries.

For the purpose of this chapter it may be worthwhile to provide a simple definition of what we mean by a 'service industry'. Quite simply a service industry is one whose 'product' is essentially intangible, which does not require manufacturing. For example, the overnight package delivery business is a service business – it uses all kinds of hardware and manufactured goods in the operation of its business, but these are not what it is selling. It is an industry that sells service – in this case the promise that your package will arrive at its destination within a certain period of time, for a fixed amount of money, and in good condition. It is typical of many service industries in that it packages its service with the addition of many peripheral elements which are designed to convince the customer that it is a superior service to that of its competitors.

THE EVOLUTION OF SERVICE INDUSTRIES

It is really only within the past twenty-five years that we have seen the emergence and tremendous growth of the service sector. And along with this growth we have seen a quantum change in the perceptions of an entire series of industries. As these perceptions have developed they have resulted in two major developments in the services sector.

The first has been the emergence of entire industries in areas which were formerly fragmented, perceived of as professions, or considered minor rather than major activities. For example, the hotel industry of twenty-five years ago was small-scale, relatively lacking in professional training and standards, and barely an industry. Today due to many factors, among them the increasing globalisation of business and industry and the wider availability of travel, the hotel business has become a giant industry operating on a global scale. It is populated by huge, sophisticated corporations who apply the latest marketing and branding techniques.

A second major development, again largely fuelled by the vast changes which have occurred during the last quarter century in population demographics, standards of living, income levels and levels of education, has been the emergence of 'knowledge industries' such as communications, television, and computer software and industries supplying 'new' services which were formerly unavailable, for example drain cleaning, credit cards and packaged holidays.

Clearly if one were to compare the levels of new activity over the past twenty-five years in the manufacturing sector versus the services sector, one would see that the services revolution, and the movement of the major economies of the world towards tertiary or non-manufacturing activities, has occurred quietly and to a large extent almost without our noticing it.

THE IMPORTANCE OF BRANDING IN THE SERVICES SECTOR

As we can see in other parts of this book, the traditional branding emphasis has always been, and to an extent continues to be, on the branding of products, or manufactured goods.

The curious and, from a marketing point of view, challenging aspect of service industries is that services have no demonstrable, tangible points of difference which can trigger a customer's purchase decision in the traditional sense. Car manufacturers can develop many different models, can install manual or automatic transmissions, can offer different engine sizes providing the consumer with clear and definable choices in terms of performance, fuel economy, etc. A consumer can walk into a showroom and touch, kick, sit in, test drive or simply gaze lovingly at one or several models. The motor industry is geared to promoting its products in this matter and car dealers would be sorely disappointed if the public did not use their facilities in this way!

In the services sector, however, we have to deal with a very different set of circumstances. Imagine, for a moment, the reception one might get if one were to walk into a Hilton or Holiday Inn hotel and tell them that you plan to spend one hour in a hotel room to see whether you like it and that, providing it meets your expectations, you will buy the additional time that you require. Imagine 'test driving' a hotel room in this way!

No, the traditional methods by which we are able to select, sample, test and ultimately decide whether to purchase do not apply to services in the same way as they do to manufactured products. Consequently the pressures on the marketer of a service differ in a number of significant areas from those of a marketer of goods:

(1) The need to develop a unique and differentiated personality is paramount in the services sector. Frequently it is achieved via the 'human element' of the service. For example, what airline does not tell you that their pilots are better trained, or their stewardesses more charming or caring than those of other airlines? How else can one choose between several airlines all flying to the same destination and all flying the same planes which both leave and arrive at approximately the same time?

(2) The marketer of a service must segment and tailor his service to appeal to the specific needs of a sector of the market. Banks do this by designing their services for either the needs of the business user or the individual consumer; accounting firms can differentiate themselves and their services by developing expertise in tax accounting, or accounting for manufacturing industry, farmers, etc.

(3) One can build one's service around one or more key elements in the provision of that service, for example speed, efficiency, courtesy, cleanliness, etc.

The simple problem with all these approaches to the differentiation of services tends to be that at this level one is still dealing with 'generic' services – that is, none of these elements or ingredients is unique, for the most part, to your service relative to all the competing services in the field.

However, by using the techniques of branding, which until relatively recently had been too little used in the area of services, it is possible to begin to develop a perception in the market place of that individual personality, that unique combination of service elements and attributes which serve to set you apart from the competition. That is, to create a service brand. And in exactly the same way as Coca-Cola has developed a unique and protectable aura around its particular tangible version of syrup and carbonated water, so a similarly unique and protectable aura can be built for an intangible service. The only difference is that in the service sector the need for consistency, credibility and protectability is probably greater since there is no hard product, only intangibles such as reputation or testimonials, to back up the claims of the service provider.

Branding, in its ability to represeent the synthesis of multiple qualities or claims in a single name, offers the services sector a marketing tool of unparalleled potential.

SOME SERVICE BRANDING SUCCESS STORIES

Household drain and pipe cleaning was formerly a commodity business. When problems occurred the consumer was likely to turn to his local telephone directory, or call his neighbour, in order to find an appropriate supplier. Prior to the advent of sophisticated, marketing-oriented national chains or franchises, the answer was likely to be, for example, try 'Brown and Sons Plumbing Services', or 'Tom Smith – Drain Clearance'.

Dyno-Rod in the UK, or Roto-Rooter in the USA, are two companies who understand the value of branding in a business as fragmented as specialised plumbing services, in this case drain and pipe cleaning. Furthermore, they understand the value of such key elements in the service as trained personnel, smart and distinctive uniforms, modern, standardised equipment, vans displaying the company logo and colours, centralised order and despatch, standard rates for various levels of job or service, and guarantees of performance and workmanship, so that the customer had recourse in the event that the job was not done correctly. Backed by extensive promotion and advertising, these two companies have revolutionised an existing service and in the process built an industry.

In the 1950s every corner cafe or coffee shop sold coffee, tea, soft drinks and sandwiches. Some had limited menus, some extensive; some were clean, most were dirty; and the list of other variables was endless, including such things as price, courtesy, staffing, quality of food, locations, sanitary conditions, opening and closing hours, etc. In short, unless one returned to the same place time after time, cafes and coffee shops were an endless surprise, frequently neither pleasant nor satisfactory.

But the food industry was changing. It was developing frozen foods, new equipment, better catering packs and the result was more extensive and better menus. The development of more sophisticated equipment meant that more capital was required, leading to the need for a greater business orientation. Other key developments included more travel by car, increased eating away from the home, national road-building programmes and a greater propensity on the part of the public to try new foods.

The development of regional and national restaurant chains, many through franchising, offered the consuming public for the first time high and consistent standards of food at value for money prices. The benefits to the public were enormous and those pioneeering companies prepared to apply the principles of mass production, quality control, personnel training, sophisticated marketing and extensive advertising and promotion have enjoyed enormous success. And as with the drain and pipe-cleaning companies, the key qualities and attributes of all of these companies reside in their names – from Topeka to Tokyo, and from Newcastle to Nantes, the names of McDonalds, Wimpy, Burger King and Kentucky Fried Chicken need no explanation, for the world knows that they stand for clean, predictable and fast service and for quality and price levels that no Joe's Coffee Shop or Stadium Cafe would ever achieve.

SERVICES BRANDING – A NEW CONSUMER BENEFIT

The world of service industries is now full of established and emerging examples of what we have come to expect from the world of manufactured goods – branded products embracing attributes of quality, consistency, availability and pricing, represented by a brand name. Both service industries and the public are finally learning that one does not necessarily have to have a manufactured product to achieve uniform standards of quality. Services or service products can be packaged, branded, advertised and promoted in very much the same way as tangible goods, though they have the key difference that they all involve one important and variable ingredient – the human ingredient. The key advantage to the consumer which the branding of services provides is that for the first time the consumer now has an identifiable, reliable and recognisable service, represented by the brand. He is thus able to judge with confidence the relative value of the service and whether to repeat the purchase or switch to an alternative service. He knows what to expect, and what he should be getting for his money.

Such service areas as catering, travel, package delivery, speciality printing and retailing have learned the value of service brands. Other areas, particularly the providers of financial services, are just waking up to branding through deregulation and the explosion in the use of credit cards, ACT's and specialist savings plans imply that the financial services sector will necessarily have to learn about branding fast. Yet other areas – specialised medical services, home improvement services, legal services and many more – still represent virgin territory for the marketer ready to apply the techniques of branding.

13 Branding in the Pharmaceutical Industry

BARBARA SUDOVAR

THE RISE OF THE GENERIC DRUG

The entire pharmaceutical industry has gone through a major transformation in the past ten years. Some healthcare professionals who have lived through this period consider it a great experience: many, however, consider it to be a grave misfortune. Certainly the 'drug industry', as it is so irreverently referred to by the layman, has entered a new era. It will never again return to its state of some ten years ago.

The transformation referred to is the dawning of 'generic drugs', which took place in the early 1970s all over the world and not just in the United States. This new era of drug manufacturing is changing the entire industry's methods and strategies for successfully marketing ethical or prescription drug products. In order to understand the rôle of trademarks in this unusual but fascinating industry, one must first understand this transition.

The advent of generic drug manufacturing and marketing has meant that almost everything a major drug manufacturer has done in the past, in terms of marketing strategies and tactics, has now to be accomplished by entirely different means so as to protect the drug and the original manufacturer's rights. Many marketing plans now have to be changed in order successfully to combat this new unknown competition in the market place – the 'generic drug'. However, no one could definitely project the future impact the generic manufacturer could or would have on the industry as a whole. This unknown factor has proved for the pharmaceutical industry to be the most significant event, or indeed crisis, of the decade. The dawning of the generic drug has led to the entire transformation of a worldwide business.

The generic drug has, for a variety of reasons, eventually proved very successful, though not in a way one might have anticipated from the outset. Today, in the mid-1980s, the generic product has infiltrated almost every category. Gone are the times when manufacturers could rely on their patents to gain some protection for their discoveries and investments. Hence the

130

increasing importance of trademarks to the pharmaceutical industry.

Before the advent of generic drugs, pharmaceutical trademarks were often representative or semi-descriptive of a drug class or even a specific drug compound. For example, an ampicillin drug was given the trade-name Polycillin, and amoxicillin became Amoxil. Many of the early antibiotics, often penicillins, were given names which would indicate that they were in fact pencillins – Vibramycin, Terramycin and Cleocin. Even today, in the mid 1980s, many pharmaceutical companies continue to use a similar method of trademarking drug products. They are trying to develop proprietary names from the generic names. Further examples of this are as follows: the generic ticarcillin has the trade-name Ticar, piperacillin has the trade-name of Pipracil, mezlocillin has the trade-name Mezlin, and azlocillin has the trade-name Azlin. However, there is now emerging a new approach to the branding of pharmaceutical products, namely, that a company should attempt to both distinguish and separate its proprietary products from what the industry considers the intruders – the generic products – by developing brand names which are far removed from the generic names, that are distinctive, unique and difficult to imitate.

MAKING IT TOO EASY FOR THE GENERICS

Years ago when a drug went off patent, seventeen years or so after it was first invented, a company did not have to worry that some other company might copy their product . . . because they would not. Today, after the patent expires, a product then becomes generic and this means that the production of the exact drug compound by a competitive company is no longer prohibited by law. Therefore, anyone with a drug corporation licence, on the day the patent expires on a drug compound, is legally able to manufacture that drug compound simply by requesting a copy of the section of the NDA (New Drug Application) submission file where the manufacturing specifications of the drug compound are described, as all that information becomes public knowledge at the time a compound becomes generic. In fact, to make things even easier the government now requires only that generic companies submit abbreviated NDAs – based upon the research trials and experience of the company that invented the drug. A generic compound does not even need a trade-name. Indeed, all that most physicians and pharmacists learn during their education are the generic names of drug compounds, not the trade-names. The reasoning behind such wide use of the generic name for a drug compound is simply to make it that much easier for a pharmacist to substitute a generic compound for a branded product. This is where all the problems and confusion begin. When a company's drug goes off patent they want to be able to protect the investment, franchise and reputation of the product that they worked so hard to create, and on which they may have spent hundreds of millions of dollars. If a trademark is easily copied or too closely identified with the generic name the major pharmaceutical company has lost the battle before it has even begun to fight.

You might ask yourself why. The answer is because the closer your trade-name or brand name is to the generic name or the medical category to which the compound belongs (such as Amoxil, the trade-name for a compound referred to as amoxicillin), the more difficult the trademark is to protect in a court of law. Thus, it is that much easier for pharmacists to substitute one drug for another without the patient ever knowing it.

We should address ourselves at this stage to the question of why pharmacists want to use generic drugs and, further, why companies want to make generic drugs. I am sure you already know the answer – to make money. The old 'profit motive' all over again. The question I would like to address, however, is how do generic companies accomplish this goal in the pharmaceutical business and what are the risks involved in allowing these companies to do so?

Let us start with the first part of that question. Generic companies are able to manufacture a drug by using the specifications that the originator filed with the Food and Drug Administration in the NDA or New Drug Application. As previously mentioned, this becomes public knowledge at the time of patent expiration. In turn, they are also able to manufacture a product cheaper than the originator of the drug compound and this allows them to sell the drug cheaper in the marketplace. Let me explain. First, the generic drug manufacturer does not have the clinical development costs associated with developing a drug compound, since he merely cites the clinical efficacy shown and documented in the originator's NDA file. Secondly, the generic drug manufacturer does not have the same stringent quality control standards the major corporations are obliged to function under. (This is one method that governments use to keep the large healthcare corporations under control.) Thirdly, the generic drug manufacturer does not have the new drug research expenditures which the major pharmaceutical corporations have. All these reasons account for the major portion of the cost of a drug. Obviously, without these overhead expenses, a generic drug can be sold more cheaply than the originator's drug and still make a decent profit.

SO WHAT'S WRONG WITH GENERICS?

To put a new drug on the market today, in the mid-1980s, could cost a pharmaceutical drug manufacturer anywhere from $15 to $50 million. It is difficult for most of us to imagine what 50 million dollars represents. In the drug business, this will pay for all those clinical studies (both animal and human) which are required, as well as any additional studies that the FDA requires prior to the approval of a drug product. Also, the original drug company will continue to perform post-marketing surveillance studies (not included in the dollar amount previously stated) which encompass continued monitoring of the drug as well as continued drug studies after the product is being sold, in order to be sure it does not become in any way a health hazard. (For example, this is how the Lilly drug Oraflex and the McNeil drug Zomax were both found to have health hazards; they were subsequently withdrawn from the market voluntarily by the individual drug companies.) One should also remember that this enormous sum does not pay for the original drug advertising and promotion to doctors or for drug sampling, a procedure whereby doctors may trial test the drug on specific patients for efficacy in order to understand the drug in-depth before prescribing the product to their widespread patent population. But rather, these promotional expenses are included in the company's first year marketing costs and not in the development budget.

Further, one must realise that small generic houses do not spend money on continued scientific research into new pharmaceutical compounds, as do the large ethical pharmaceutical companies. One must further understand that much of the profit which major companies earn from their marketed drugs is ploughed back into research. Without these large companies footing the bill to develop new products to combat old and new illnesses, if in fact we were all to depend on the generic houses, we would never see another new drug compound introduced again. This is the truth! All that the generic manufacturers do is manufacture generic or patent expired drugs. Never would there be any new drugs – only old, patent expired drugs. Where would we be today without beta blockers, tricyclic antidepressants, phenothiazines and the like? sants, phenothiazines and the like?

Many of the major pharmaceutical companies continue to sell their drugs after the patents have expired in the hope of gaining additional income to pay for more new product development. But many drug products never in fact pass the break-even point. They never earn a return. There is a serious flaw in the regulatory process whereby a company must patent a drug compound at the time it believes it to be a new discovery. Thereafter, the development process often takes ten to twelve years leaving perhaps seven or sometimes only five years of patent-life before the drug becomes generic. It generally takes a drug company at least four to five years to recoup its investment on that new drug product leaving at most two or three years actually to make money on the drug.

It follows too that by allowing generic companies to manufacture patent-expired drugs patients may be put at risk, especially those who are chronically ill. That is, those patients who have an illness which will, in most cases, stay with them for their entire lives. Examples would be diabetes, asthma, high blood pressure, heart disease, and so on. For such patients who have been taking a specific drug for many years a switch to a generic drug could be highly detrimental. Let me explain. The patient has been stabilised on a certain drug and one day he or she is given a generic drug prescription because the patent expired on the drug product they were taking. The generic product is supposed to be therapeutically and biochemically identical. However, this may not prove in fact to be the case. The patient consumes the product and their body (for whatever reason) rejects it. If the patient has a severe heart condition this could kill them. Why has this happened? So that some person could save a little money on a drug prescription that may or may not be equivalent to the original drug they were taking. A chronically ill patient needs to be standardised on a drug, a diet, a lifestyle and maybe all three. To change any or all of these components is merely asking for trouble and placing the chronically ill patient in unnecessary danger. Now, at this point, it is my hope that you understand, to some degree, the significance of the rôle generic drug manufacturing plays in the pharmaceutical industry.

We can now move on to the matter to trademarks in the pharmaceutical industry since we have fully examined the one event which has dramatically changed the entire industry's thinking as well as its future.

IMPORTANCE OF STRONG BRAND NAMES

One of the most significant changes in the industry has been the growing use of strong trade-names on new drug products. As mentioned before, in the past trade names have generally reflected the generic compound but today trademarks are becoming much more innovative. Two recent trade-names which stand out as excellent examples of this process and which happen to be in competition with even each other are: the anti-ulcer drug product sold by SmithKline branded Tagamet but with the generic name of cimetidine and, secondly, another anti-ulcer agent sold by Glaxo-Roche with the branded name Zantac and a generic name of ranitidine. Neither of these branded trade names bears any relationship to the generic name and this is great. This innovative approach allows both trade-names to be more easily protected by law and also discourages generic intrusion through the use of substitution. In addition, you can see that these trade-names are very creative and different yet are not difficult to pronounce, write or spell – very important criteria for a good drug trademark. Since the physician will have to write and pronounce the trade-name many times in his daily routine, a company must make the trademark as easy to remember as it is to spell and pronounce. These are three very important priorities in the development of trade-names which will help make them successful.

The commercial importance of this type of innovative branding can perhaps best be illustrated by one fact. Tagamet recently became the first $1 billion drug in history – the serious intrusion of a generic equivalent when this drug goes off patent could quite literally devastate its owner and inventor SmithKline.

Another trademark philosophy which has surfaced with the advent of generics has been the development of trade-names indicative of what disease the product is useful in treating. For example, in recent years a product has been developed for use in heart disease. The product was branded Procardia, Pro- meaning 'for' and -cardia indicating that the drug should be used for patients with heart problems. Another example of a trade-name indicating the use of a drug is Glucotrol, indicating glucose control for the diabetic patient. These are, in my opinion, two powerful examples of pre-emptive pharmaceutical branding – differentiated, international and a 'tough act' for other pharmaceutical and generic companies to follow.

INTERNATIONAL BRANDS

There are several methods of establishing strong trademark franchises in the pharmaceutical industry. A relatively new philosophy is to try to establish an indentical trademark all over the world. One must emphasise the word 'try' because companies are not always successful in registering the same trademark for a specific product all over the world. Many of the major pharmaceutical companies operate in fifty or more countries around the world. This presents a problem in that what may seem to be a good name for a product in English may be a totally unacceptable name in another language. Sometimes only a letter or two will have to be changed in one or two languages to solve the problem and in effect the trade-name will be seen as a worldwide trademark. However, this is not always the case. When the exact trade-name cannot be used in three or more of the major pharmaceutical markets of the world (US, UK, Italy, France, Germany, Japan, Spain, Switzerland, Sweden, Holland or Austria) then a different trademark may have to be chosen.

The technique of developing a worldwide trademark is very complex but can be well worth the effort, particularly in the event of any future trademark infringement cases. If a trademark has been established on a worldwide basis, the ownership of it and rights to it are much more protectable.

Further, a worldwide trademark ensures familiarity with the trade-name and with the product, as well as with the manufacturer because the trade-name is the same all over the world. The combination of an innovative, worldwide trademark makes for an exceptional marketing and legal product franchise.

CREATING NEW BRANDS

The most common methodology employed in pharmaceutical companies which have international divisions is to first create a trademark that is acceptable in the domestic market-place – frequently the USA – and only then, after registrability is established, will the name be checked for availability and suitability in other countries of the world. The reasoning behind this action is simple. The United States, for example, represents about one-third of the world in terms of worldwide pharmaceutical sales, Japan represents another third and the rest of the world represents the final third. Clearly, therefore, the United States and Japan are most likely to be the two nations which are most important to any international pharmaceutical corporation.

As has been pointed out, there are several new emerging strategies being employed in the development of international pharmaceutical trademarks and each company must decide which method is best for its situation. Many corporations have established what are known as trademark committees. These committees are made up of several members representing various divisions of the corporation as well as various disciplines. It is the duty of the committee to recommend to upper management possible trade-names for new drugs which are suitable and which have been legally searched and found to be clear and therefore registrable all over the world.

Since the task of developing a worldwide trademark is so complex and involves considerable work, many of these committees have looked to outside agencies to develop an acceptable worldwide trademark for a specific product. These companies listen to the committee's description of a specific drug and the corporation's intended marketing position, as well as their ideas for types of prefixes or suffixes that are preferred or disliked. The agency then conducts group panels in key cities around the world to seek the preferences of doctors and consumers. They also use computer programs to develop shortlists of names for presentation to the client. Many corporations have found this method to be very satisfactory; however, the process is still quite complex, particularly when it becomes involved in the area of searching and registration of the trademarks in countries around the world. As I had mentioned previously, Japan is a very significant market for international divisions and therefore it is mandatory that a worldwide trademark be accepted in the Japanese market. Due to the great difference of the Japanese language it is advisable always to test potential names for pronunciation and use with Japanese physicians.

Another basic problem for US pharmaceutical companies in developing worldwide trademarks is that most drug products following development and clinical testing are first marketed abroad before ever being approved in the United States. This makes the process even more complex since the time constraints are much more severe internationally than they are in the USA. Therefore, most trademarks must be developed several years in advance of launching the product abroad in order to satisfy the numerous country requirements concerning trademark registrability. Therefore, the trade-name will be chosen many years in advance of the drug's approval and introduction into the US market. Agreement between the various corporate divisions (domestic and international) is often difficult to achieve in terms of a worldwide trademark, but in terms of its value to a pharmaceutical corporation it is essential to move in this direction. An excellent example of a recently developed worldwide trademark is Feldene, the trade-name for piroxicam, an anti-arthritic drug sold by Pfizer, Inc.

CONCLUSIONS

Today and for as long as generic drugs are sold, the development of trademarks for new pharmaceutical products will be one of the most important tasks facing the pharmaceutical industry. It is by no means a job that should be taken lightly, for it could very easily make or break a product when it enters the market-place.

14 Branding at Austin Rover

TERRY NOLAN

INTRODUCTION

In 1985, about 35 million cars were purchased around the world and car brands – from Mercedes to Chevrolet, from Nissan to Volvo – are some of the most pervasive brands in existence. Austin Rover, Britain's leading indigenous car manufacturer, manufactured only a small proportion of those cars built in 1985 – something over 1 per cent – yet Austin Rover's experience and problems in the tricky area of car branding is unparalleled. After all, the company is the successor to a process of merger and amalgamation going back decades and, over this period, has inherited brands, loyalties and prejudices which have provided branding opportunities and problems on an unprecedented scale.

THE MARKET

In 1985, the world's vehicle 'parc', the number of cars on the world's roads, was 365 million. By the year 2000 this figure will rise to over 500 million. There are currently 157 major manufacturers of motor cars in the world offering the world's motorists some 2700 model ranges. In 1985, in the UK alone, a market taking only about 5 per cent of the world's car manufacturing output, around £135 million was spent on media advertising. The statistics of the motor industry are staggering.

Yet the motor industry as we know it today is the result of a continuous evolution over the course of the last century. Many important car manufacturing companies, for example Studebaker, have fallen by the wayside while others have been absorbed into larger and larger groupings such as General Motors of the USA or Peugeot/Citroen/Talbot of France.

AUSTIN ROVER

Austin Rover has evolved through such a process and, in its previous incarnation, was known as British Leyland. British Leyland was formed in

1968 from the Leyland Motor Corporation and British Motor Holdings Limited and, as each of these two companies in turn comprised groupings of smaller companies, in effect some forty-two separate companies were merged together into a single entity. The result was predictable – complications arose with frequent changes of management, of policy and even of the company title. And this confusion rapidly communicated itself to the purchasing public worldwide. Even the strong loyalties inherent in the company's leading brands – among them, Austin, Rover, Triumph, MG and Jaguar – could not prevent a decline in sales, market share and profits.

Austin Rover emerged from this morass in the late 1970s with a clear brief to reverse the decline of the company and restore it to profitability. It is Britain's only major car manufacturer, one of its leading earners of foreign exchange and one of its largest employers of labour. The rescue of British Leyland by the government and the subsequent creation of Austin Rover as an aggressive and competitive volume car manufacturer was clearly of critical importance not just to creditors, customers, employees and suppliers but to the community at large.

The new management at Austin Rover introduced an ambitious programme of new product development, new marketing concepts and new manufacturing techniques and reduced manning levels in all areas of the company, thus increasing productivity enormously. Between 1979 and 1984 virtually every major product in the company's range was replaced, massive losses were reduced to a near break-even situation, Jaguar was brought to the Stock Exchange as a separate specialist car manufacturer and, in an intensely competitive market situation with massive overcapacity throughout Europe, the company's prospects were transformed.

NAMING THE COMPANY

In this environment of swift and competent change it was obviously vital that Austin Rover should review its stance in terms of establishing a meaningful company name and appropriate product brands. Very detailed investigations were made of all the company's previous passenger car marques. Considerable debate took place and not a little emotion was involved – after all, the future of the company was under discussion and many executives had close affiliations with companies which became constituent parts of the larger company.

Eventually the corporate title Austin Rover was chosen because the large volume car company attributes of Austin, together with its 'value for money' image for the family motorist, contrasted nicely with the prestigious view held in the UK and Europe of Rover as offering a little more in terms of driving and specification for a little more in price.

In making this decision the name Morris, a marque strongly associated with the large manufacturing complex at Cowley, was deleted as a company name, an action not taken lightly! Morris was extremely well known in the UK but had little history of sales abroad. Whilst it was perceived by the UK consumer as representing 'value for money', it had associations of poor quality and reliability and was also regarded as lacking in specification and modernity. Reluctantly, it had to go.

A more difficult decision was that to shelve the name Triumph. Triumph had a much stronger image than Morris but was generally thought of as being a sports car. It was well recognised around the world but overall volumes were small and spread very thinly. It was felt, therefore, to have little real image advantage for the new company so again it had to go.

At the same time such 'secondary' brands as Wolseley, Riley, Standard and Lanchester were also reviewed and discarded. These had been strong brands in their time but were generally considered to be too old fashioned to fit the image of the new technologically advanced Austin Rover Company.

Having established that Austin Rover represented the best images available from a conglomerate that had previously been known as British Leyland or Leyland Cars, it was vital that every aspect of the company's external communications be directed to project the Austin Rover image clearly to world customers. Thus a new theme was developed through corporate identity, advertising and the products themselves to identify Austin as an efficient volume car manufacturer offering value for money for the family motorist and Rover as a car manufacturer offering prestigious motoring for those who wanted a little more. These two marques, when combined as Austin Rover, were to project a new image of a company selling British cars worldwide.

NAMING THE METRO

The launch, in 1979, of the new car coded LC8 – a small hatchback vehicle designed to sell alongside the Mini – heralded for the first time a realisation within the company of the real problems that lie behind product branding. Up until that time management felt that the Society of Motor Manufacturers and Traders' roster of brand names had sufficient data to fulfil all the future needs of Austin Rover. It transpired that most of the names on the roster assigned to Austin Rover were unsuitable for our purposes and some of the reserved names had, in fact, been taken and used by other motor manufacturers, who were either not party to the industry-wide agreements or chose to ignore them.

Austin Rover thus found themselves with literally dozens of well-established range and model names, all of which were felt to be unsuitable for use on a new and exciting car. Hence the need, despite a superabundance of existing names in the company's 'name bank', to develop a new name for LC8.

In some ways it is understandable that the company should put a high priority on the name. After all, if the car was unsuccessful this could call into question Austin Rover's future. The car had been designed, all styling features agreed, even the colour schemes were fixed for the first year or so after launch, yet choosing a new name proved to be extremely difficult.

As my responsibilities included long-range plans, for some reason the task of developing a name for LC8, acceptable to consumers on an international basis and legally available, fell to me.

My initial shock was to find that old brands are not necessarily sacrosanct in the SMM and T International Names Register and this propelled me into a frenzy of activity. First of all, we prepared a 'word picture' (photographs were disallowed for security reasons) of the new small car identifying salient selling attributes, the competition and the target sales levels required. Armed with this data I visited all four of our advertising agencies (Leyland Cars, as it was still known at that time, included Austin, Rover, Morris, Triumph, Jaguar, Land-Rover and Range Rover products). I also visited a new company in London offering a product-naming service called Novamark International. The advertising agencies let their imaginations run riot, as did the public for it had become general knowledge that we had yet to resolve the naming issue. Robert Glenton wrote an article in the *Sunday Express* on 4 March 1979, stating: 'Leyland's are scratching their poor little heads trying to think of a new name for the latest Mini of theirs (if they ever build it). Perhaps you would like to write in to them and give them your advice?'

Already the combined efforts of our employees, our advertising agents and members of he public had produced a list of many thousands of potential names and these we passed to Novamark. Novamark used consumer creation groups, copywriters and their computer name generation programs to develop thousands more.

It soon emerged from the creation work, however, that consumers, particularly in Britain, required more than just an attractive and appropriate name for the new car. In investment terms the LC8 project represented one of the largest single industrial investments ever made in Britain and the necessary funds were being provided as loans by the government. These funds were being used not just for development purposes but to build and equip one of the most advanced and efficient car manufacturing plants in Europe. Public interest in the project was intense. Considerable scepticism remained as to the likely success of LC8 but all eyes were focused on it.

In branding terms it became increasingly clear that our task was not just one of branding the new car but, rather, of developing a branding strategy that was so coherent and sensible that it would signal to consumers that the company itself was operating along coherent and sensible lines. Research had shown that consumers saw the disarray in the company's naming policies in the recent past (brands included Princess, Dolomite, Marina and dozens of others) as simply being a reflection of the overall confusion within the company.

I cannot claim that this realisation of the need to develop an overall branding strategy for the Austin range rather than a single name was a sudden inspiration. Rather, it was a requirement which emerged gradually though it was prompted initially by the consumer groups held by Novamark. Once we started considering the implications, we looked first at the branding strategies adopted by our competitors and few of them had really solved the problem either. Companies like Mercedes and BMW used an alpha-numeric system quite effectively, Volkswagen had taken the 'wind' route with only mixed success (for example the Scirocco and Passat), and Fiat simply used a numbering sequence based upon development project numbers which sometimes left the consumer baffled!

Our task, then, was to find a branding approach which would work well on LC8 but could be applied equally well to all future volume car models (and two were due to be launched in fairly short succession) so that over time a line-up of brands would develop which consumers would see as being sensible, logical and attractive and which, consciously or unconsciously, would lead them to acknowledge that Austin Rover had 'got its act together'. We looked at developing sequences of names based on Greek gods, planets, oceans, birds, animals, even precious stones. All these routes had their attractions but all had profound problems – there are only so many attractive birds, animals or Greek gods to go round, many had already been taken, they often do not translate successfully from one language to another and we did not want to find ourselves naming a new car the Wildebeest or the Gnu because it was the only animal left on which we could obtain legal clearance!

So for a time a logical sequence eluded us and we continued to develop names where their main unifying feature was that they were short, attractive and international. However, we were aware that the only model in the line-up, at that time, likely to survive the introduction of the new volume car models was the Mini, so obviously the name Mini had to be integrated somehow into the new naming strategy. Gradually it dawned on us that the simplest and most elegant solution to our problem was to give all the new models names beginning with M—. In this way Mini would be properly integrated into the new naming sequence, we had an overt and very simple unifying theme, yet there was no problem in finding names with international acceptability and/or availability, nor was there ever any danger of our running out of names.

This solution was emerging at a time when our initial shortlist of many thousands of names had been reduced to about fifty preferred names, many of which started with M— but not all. We were still keeping our options open and the M— strategy had not yet been put to management for approval. These fifty names were going through consumer testing, language checks and full international legal searches and we were confident that at least one name would survive by the time we reached our deadline. The legal searches in particular caused a high attrition rate. We were determined that we should use the same name on a virtually global basis, though Europe was of especial interest, and it was staggering to find how many thousands of names were already registered for cars, automotive components, tyres, car hire services, etc., and hence how many of our preferred names fell by the wayside.

Eventually, about a month before our deadline, we had reduced our list of fifty names to just six – four M— names and two others. None of these names was totally clear at that time in all countries, but the problems appeared to be relatively minor ones and our trademark lawyers were confident that, with a little time, one and perhaps two names could be unscrambled.

That is when the Chairman, Sir Michael Edwardes, dropped his bombshell!

There was very little enthusiasm on my part – or for that matter on Novamark's – when Sir Michael issued an edict that he required within a very short time not just one but three attractive names for the car, all fully cleared, so that the workforce could be involved in choosing the name of the new 'Mighty Mini'. This was, of course, a brilliant workforce relations exercise but there were a number of very pale faces in the Marketing and Legal Departments at the prospect of finding three good, strong, protectable names in so short a time. Fortunately we all survived and the poll of the workers duly took place. Voting was close:

METRO 8599 votes
MAESTRO   8332 votes

and MATCH, most favoured in Europe, fell away quite sharply.

It is noticeable that, perhaps by good fortune (though there was a little more to it than that), all three names put to the workforce ballot started with M—. The new branding strategy was beginning to emerge.

FURTHER NAMING PROBLEMS

In the first five years after the Metro was launched almost 750 000 cars were sold. For two years in succession it was Britain's best selling small car. It allowed Austin Rover to survive as a volume car producer. So much for Robert Glenton's comment, in March 1979, 'if they ever build it'.

In the years after the launch of Metro the company turned its attention to a new five-door hatchback saloon and, later, a larger four-door saloon and estate car. These were named, respectively, Maestro and Montego. It is interesting that the development of the four M's naming strategy – Mini, Metro, Maestro and Montego – in a sense crept up on the company. Up to this time the importance of the brand or model name was well recognised, and indeed it was this recognition which led management to debate endlessly the naming of new cars. But the process was seen essentially as a 'Eureka' process – somewhere out there is the perfect name for this new car and I shall recognise it when I see it.

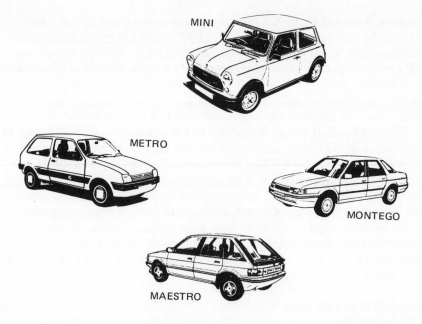

FIGURE 14.1　*The Four Ms*

Indeed, when we first went to Novamark it was really because 'Eureka' was somehow just eluding us; we saw their rôle as essentially being that of wordsmiths.

In the event, we now have a naming strategy for volume cars which will serve us well for the foreseeable future, which enormously simplifies all naming decisions and which is recognised and liked by consumers. It was, however, only in the two to three years after the launch of Metro that the Four M naming strategy was really accepted and internalised throughout the company. It is apparent that a naming issue can be a very passionate problem, and even simple, elegant naming solutions are not necessarily immediately accepted.

Having decided the branding philosophy for the Austin volume car products, it seemed sensible for Rover products to be differentiated away from the Austin branding route, especially if they were to be marketed in the same sectors. This approach cuts down substitutional sales between Austin Rover customers and promotes conquest or company growth. Earlier it has become evident that the Triumph Acclaim was to be replaced and the Triumph marque discontinued, and in an effort to make the replacement car – produced in the UK but of a basic design originated by Honda – completely different from the Honda vehicles, it was our view that we should identify the new car as a Rover.

FIGURE 14.2　*The Rover 200 series*

Research had shown that, in Britain in particular, the name Rover still stood for prestige motoring. Owners of large Rover cars were not unhappy with the Rover name being used on smaller vehicles, provided these vehicles retained the concept of prestige motoring. We rejected any consideration of adopting model names for Rover, the approach used for Austin, but we were keen to differentiate the two ranges. Therefore a numeric branding approach was adopted for Rover that would make the prestige Rover name work harder and help maintain the Austin and Rover range differential. We were obviously not unaware that other manufacturers of prestige cars tended to follow the numerical approach; hence this would further signal to consumers that Rover cars were prestigious.

In fact the decision to go 'small Rover' took much soul-searching and critical analysis of the product in terms of engineering excellence, ride and, of course, the specifications that Rover owners would expect. Management and workers alike met the challenge and we now find that demand is outstripping supply.

MODEL DERIVATIVES

The final phase of the naming conundrum was the complicated problem of identifying the derivatives of our basic model ranges. As mentioned earlier, there are some 2700 model ranges worldwide and many of these have six or more derivatives to each range.

Our Metro 'character model' approach helped to reduce the complexities:

INEXPENSIVE	FUNCTIONAL	ECONOMY
Metro City	Metro 'L'	Metro LE/HLE
Second car purchase	Broad appeal	58.3 mpg at 56 mph
First time buyer	Top selling derivative	

PERFORMANCE PLUS	HIGH LUXURY
Metro MG/Turbo	Metro Vanden Plas
0–60 9 secs.	Top of the range
Max speed 112 mph	

'City' was adopted for our lower line models. 'MG' – a marque originally well known in the period 1960–70 and derived from 'Morris Garage' – was adopted as a very strong sports derivative by Austin. (Do you remember the hue and cry from MG enthusiasts when we decided to use this name for a small 'runabout' like the Metro? Well, we have now sold more Metro MGs than we ever sold MGB GT tourers, etc.!)

Another strong but slightly old-fashioned marque was adopted for a luxury version – the Metro Vanden Plas – a little long as a name and a little dated perhaps but well known in coachbuilding circles. However, the key attributes of these strong derivative titles was their ability to develop acceptable styling cues that the public could recognise.

STYLING CUES

MG	VANDEN PLAS
High speed, fast acceleration	Refined driving
Red piping to seating	Real walnut wood facing
Matching red seat belts	Leather available
Red carpets	Top specification including latest in-car-entertainment, electric windows, etc.
MG octagon on wheel trims, steering wheel and on front/rear of the car	The Vanden Plas badge inscribed on steering wheel, road wheels and on the car – front & rear.

At Austin Rover we have worked towards a continuity of naming and titles like Vanden Plas and MG appear on all four 'M' Austin ranges.

For Rover too the same simple approach is followed with continuity of this basic logic. Vanden Plas, the sign of luxury driving, appears on both Austin and Rover models. Rover, however, have adopted the name Vitesse to signify performance, leaving MG with Austin.

CONCLUSIONS

The first phase of our product rationalisation is now complete. We have established a reasoned approach to the company title. We have a competitive range of cars all identified, in the case of Austin, with names and, with Rover, by a numerical system. The names of our cars have, moreover, been carried through to the identity of dealers and Austin and Rover both appear in the title of the company.

However, the job ahead is as large as the job so far successfully completed. We need to grow, in fact we must double in size and this means carrying forward the Austin Rover ideals to as wide a number of consumers as possible. We can achieve this by retaining the loyalty of past customers. As we launch new models we have the oppotunity to win new customers. We are not complacent about the task ahead. Branding has played and will continue to play an important rôle in the success of the company and its emergence as a new force.

15 The Wide World of Branding

TERRY OLIVER

INTRODUCTION

Much of this book is about the development and protection of global brands. However, it is important to recognise that at the present time most brands are not world brands at all – they are national brands that occupy a particular local niche and function only in their home markets. Such local brands fall into two categories:

(1) Brands which are similar to other brands in other countries in terms of formulation, function and appearance but which for a number of reasons – for example, tariff barriers, established competition in overseas markets, trademark problems or lack of interest on the part of their owners – are not sold outside their home markets.
(2) Brands which are so idiosyncratically adapted to their home markets that they are unlikely to have immediate appeal in foreign markets.

Brands which fall into this first category are by far the most common. In Britain, for example, bread is heavily branded but the major varieties are at most national in their scope. The difficulties involved in the export of fresh food, together with such factors as local tastes, largely account for the localised nature of brands in this segment.

Idiosyncratic local brands include many Japanese foods which generally do not appeal to non-Japanese palates; products such as English ales which frequently do not appeal to consumers brought up on the lighter, more carbonated beers and yeast extracts such as Marmite (from Britain) and its Australian 'cousin' Vegemite – such yeast-based products are used as savoury spreads and enjoy enormous popularity in their home markets, but are considered decidedly odd by those not brought up to appreciate their rather subtle appeals.

148

It is, therefore, clearly possible to develop large, strong and successful local brands based entirely upon local markets – indeed most brands are of this type. It is, though, apparent that such brands are increasingly overshadowed by the major international brands which are seen to have more power, more appeal and are altogether more reassuring to the consumer. Although consumers support their local brands, there is an undeniable attraction to the 'big' brand which is frequently of international or global standing.

But need local brands necessarily remain local? Does not the fact that a product is found appealing in one market tend to suggest that there could be other markets out there which might find it equally appealing? It is interesting to note that in the United States the enormous growth of the ethnic food market and the general broadening of eating habits have created niche markets for many foreign products, which were formerly purely local brands. The range of imported beers and foods to be found in the supermarkets of the major cities would have been inconceivable even five years ago. And this phenomenon is not confined to the United States. European brewers, for example, have penetrated both the US and the UK markets with enormous success, and beer drinkers, particularly the younger and more upwardly mobile ones, have adjusted their tastes and switched to imports with increasing frequency. Yet neither the British nor the American brewers have responded to this phenomenon by establishing, at least until recently, any real presence outside their home markets. American brewers were so confident about the anticipated endless growth of their own domestic market that they almost totally ignored the booming markets of Western Europe and Japan – until the growth at home stopped and they discovered that significant pieces of their domestic market had been poached from under their noses by their Continental European, Japanese, Mexican and Canadian competitors. British brewers too have done little to exploit overseas markets, yet in their dark beers and ales they have unique products which could well have a wider appeal. Trade regulations and other 'market imperfections' undoubtedly hinder or even prevent the development of foreign or overseas markets. However, one suspects that in many cases the real reason for local brands not becoming world brands is more likely to be lack of enterprise, lack of commitment and the failure to spot opportunity before it is too late rather than the fact that the products are unacceptable outside home markets or because of governmental interference.

Nevertheless, while markets draw closer together and become similar, it is important that we continue to be aware of national particularities. We know that Japan is a fundamentally different culture from that of most Western societies. We know too that national caricatures at times contain more than a grain of truth – brash Americans, conservative Englishmen, unco-operative French, volatile Italians, pedantic Germans and unfathomable Japanese – and in branding we need to see very clearly the differences as well as the similarities.

THE AMERICAN APPROACH TO BRANDING

With 220 million increasingly wealthy consumers, the United States frequently represents one half or more of the world's potential for any branded product. It is not surprising therefore that US corporations have frequently tended in the past to focus almost exclusively on their home market and to view the rest of the world's markets as of secondary importance. During the 1950s and 1960s this corporate myopia cost American indutry little – Western Europe, for example, was struggling to emerge from the devastation of the war. Add to this scenario the wide variety of cultures, languages and governments in Europe and it is not surprising that for many American companies Western Europe was not a particularly inviting market.

Nor did the Far East appear particularly attractive. Per capita incomes were low, tastes were radically different and in many cases unsophisticated, and the abilities of governments in the region to put road-blocks in the way of Western businesses were legendary.

As a consequence there was a strong tendency on the part of American companies to concern themselves simply with their own domestic market. As far as branding is concerned this manifested itself in a peculiarly American approach, the essence of which is directness – even bluntness.

American branding philosophy required that the brand owner get to the point as quickly as possible. Subtlety, style and gentle persuasion took a back seat to getting the message across with maximum impact, speed and efficiency. Given the sheer physical size of the US market, the enormous amount of noise made by competing products and the awesome cost involved in reaching a target market of any appreciable size, this approach to branding is understandable and, probably, appropriate. Furthermore, trademark law in the USA allowed, and still allows, companies to protect such highly direct and even descriptive brands as, for example, Dial-a-Lash for mascara, Lite for beer and HandiWrap for a food wrapping product.

The drawbacks of this approach to branding began to manifest themselves when international markets entered the picture. The US brand names frequently proved to be too descriptive to be readily protected in certain countries, for example the UK or Germany, too lacking in subtlety and non-tangible values in others, for example France and Italy, and culturally unacceptable or impossible to pronounce in others.

In a sense, the American approach to branding at times matches the national caricature and American corporations are frequently much less international in their outlook and much less sensitive in their approach to international branding than their size and the scale of their international operations might suggest.

Does this not suggest that the American approach to international branding needs some adjustment? The answer to this must be yes – and this change is already under way. US business has already adjusted to the shock brought on by the realisation of its dependency on foreign oil and to the import threats to basic industries. The joint venture between General Motors and Toyota to produce small cars is one manifestation of what is happening in electronics, steel, chemical, pharmaceuticals, retailing and banking.

Do such alliances mean that America is becoming a second-rate economic power? We do not think so. We think they simply signal a narrowing of the gap in international living standards, technology and management that we spoke about earlier in this chapter. This process creates global markets that crave similar products, that have similar aspirations and that have the wherewithal to buy and enjoy a remarkably similar range of products and services. As businesses not only in the USA but increasingly also in Britain, France, West Germany, Italy and Japan pursue global markets, international alliances represent one way to reduce risk, minimise costs and remove cultural barriers. This process in turn is leading US corporations increasingly towards international branding and a more sensitive approach to international brands.

People in the United States are accustomed to self-sufficiency so greater interdependence naturally causes some resentment. The huge American lead in technology and living standards began to be eroded during the 1960s, and now the flow of technology, ideas and products is becoming increasingly two-way. Furthermore, since the countries of Western Europe and Asia have been involved in global marketing for many more years than the USA, there is every reason to believe that America has some catching up to do in both awareness and skills. Just as foreign companies have invaded the American market with outstanding success, so must American companies invade foreign markets. Coca-Cola, Kodak, Johnson Wax and a host of others have shown the way but in many respects they still remain untypical.

THE JAPANESE APPROACH

The Japanese consumer is perfectly happy to eat Germ bread, while drinking Blendy coffee laced with Creap non-dairy creamer. He wears Trim Pecker trousers, uses Blow Up hairspray and puts Skinababe on the baby's bottom. He eats at restaurants with names like My Dung and Le Macquereau (The Pimp), and cultivates his garden with Green Pile fertiliser. The branding vocabulary in Japan is in a class by itself.

The Japanese term for words borrowed from other languages is *gairago*: the language has thousands of these borrowings, and adds hundreds more each year. However, these words are in a sense absorbed into the Japanese language, defined and written in the syllabic alphabet called *Katakana*. Loanwords in this category have their uses in consumer marketing, but it is the unadulterated gairago – the brand names and slogans in their original Roman spellings – that really move the merchandise. They get attached to cars and soft drinks and toiletries with an exuberance unmatched anywhere in the world.

The use of gairago is not a recent trend. The first product in Japan with a foreign name was a pharmaceutical called Kindorusan, introduced in the 1860s. The name itself was a hybrid. Kindoru- was written in katakana, while the -san suffix used the Chinese character for powder. The label, however, showed a picture of an elderly, heavily bearded gentleman carrying a child in a kimono, thus unequivocably proclaiming Kindorusan to be an imported or foreign product. Having just emerged at this time from a long period of self-imposed isolation, the Japanese were unable to match the quality, innovative-ness and sophistication of the foreign goods that were beginning to appear on the market. Hence foreign goods developed a distinct cachet and by extension any product with a foreign name came to have a special appeal, a mystique, an implied presumption of quality.

Although the increasingly sophisticated Japanese consumer has come to realise that foreign products are, in terms of quality, now quite often inferior to those produced domestically, foreign language brand names have lost none of their appeal and mystique. However, with the high exposure of Japanese products in foreign markets, coupled with the huge numbers of overseas visitors coming to Japan each year, companies are finding that they must be increasingly careful in the selection of brand names in languages other than their own.

Typically brand names have been created in-house by staff who were foreign language graduates or who have worked in an overseas branch of the company. In a market-place where legal peculiarities have resulted in over 1.7 million registered trademarks, and an additional 130 000 applications for registration each year, the creation of protectable and appropriate brand names for the domestic market has become extremely difficult, and finding a brand name that will also satisfy the additional requirements of foreign markets near impossible.

Although the techniques used in Japan for developing brand names are similar to those used in other countries, special problems arise in the way that Japanese consumers relate to foreign brand names. The meaning of the word, unless it happens to fall within the rather limited foreign vocabulary that most Japanese retain from their school days, is not of primary importance. The reaction the word evokes, and the way it sounds when written in Katakana are of much greater importance. The explanation that the Japanese give for this is that they are a very visually oriented people, inclined to make decisions based on emotional rather than purely logical grounds. Thus the goal of branding, and indeed of a great deal of Japanese advertising, is to create an emotional bond between the consumer and the product.

Recognising the difficulties inherent in creating foreign language brand names for use in overseas markets, a number of Japanese companies have recently used Japanese names for export products. Notable successes include Shiseido's Zen fragrance and the Katana (Sword) motor-cycle from Suzuki. However, it is unlikely that we will see any significant increase in the use of Japanese language brand names in foreign markets by Japanese companies. Although Japanese manufacturers would naturally prefer to use the same name in both domestic and foreign markets, the predilection of the Japanese consumer for foreign names, regardless of whether such names convey any message or make any logical sense, makes it unlikely that we shall see a rush of products from Japan bearing Japanese names.

There is also one further reason why Japanese companies frequently prefer foreign language brand names and it is a practical one. Japan uses three different written languages – *Kanji*, with its several thousand Chinese characters, and two phonetic systems, *Hiragana* and *Katakana*, with approximately fifty symbols in each. Katakana is used for words of foreign derivation and products with a foreign name normally carry the Katakana transliteration. Although almost all Japanese have memorised the approximately 2000 Kanji characters, this does not mean that one is able to pronounce the many combinations. Hence the use of Kanji can result in extreme confusion as to the pronunciation of the name. Therefore the use of foreign names in their Katakana transliteration ensures that confusion as to pronunciation will not be a problem.

A problem that will continue to plague Japanese manufacturers, however, is how to accommodate the vastly different branding requirements of the domestic and overseas markets. Despite the high visibility of Japanese products in world markets, it is the domestic market which continues to be of paramount importance. Products are almost always launched in the domestic market first, and those that succeed are then taken overseas. It is often at this point that problems with brand names first appear. Lack of originality often means that the name is unavailable in the markets of interest. Those that are available are frequently so idiosyncratic as to be unusable.

Pocari Sweat is a sports drink (a soft drink containing electrolytes, etc. for use after exercise) which was introduced on the Japanese market in 1980. By 1984 it had gained a 36 per cent share of the market in Japan, and generated considerable competitive interest and response from manufacturers such as Suntory and Coca-Cola. Obviously to the Japanese consumer there was nothing particularly strange or unusual in drinking a beverage called Sweat. When test-marketed overseas, however, the response was predictable and ranged from hilarity to repulsion. Naturally, although somewhat reluctantly, the name had to be changed and the product is marketed overseas as Pocari.

The challenge for Japanese companies in the future will be to identify those products which are likely to be marketed overseas at an earlier stage in their development, and to develop branding strategies which will take into consideration the diverse requirements of both the domestic and the overseas markets, allowing them to function and compete effectively in both.

THE WESTERN EUROPE APPROACH

The major Western European countries have, over the past fifteen years, provided us with the ideal laboratory in which to view the gradual move from a primarily domestic or national focus to one which is increasingly international.

European companies have traditionally been quite insular and nationalistic, and these traits have clearly manifested themselves in their approach to branding. The British, for example, have long delighted in brand names such as Oxford for cars, or Piccadilly for cigarettes. The Britishness of indigenous products has been further emphasised by the use of humour and the verbal pun in advertising and promotion.

The French, on the other hand, show such an attachment to their language and to their wish for some undefined texture in their brand names that at times they tend to develop brands which are likely to baffle even the French themselves.

Despite such national idiosyncracies the countries and companies of Western Europe have gradually been forced to adopt a wider perspective. One major influence has been the development of the European Economic Community, the Common Market as it is more usually called. This linking together of certain of the major European countries has increasingly forced companies within Western Europe to view the EEC as a single market. Freedom of movement of goods and labour has led to increased export and import activity and the growth of Eurobrands – international or multinational brands which are sold throughout Europe and sourced from multiple locations.

A further major change in the thinking of European industry has been caused by the respective sizes of the individual national markets, coupled with the economics of mass production. Essentially the individual national markets within Western Europe do not offer the necessary mass to optimise the benefits of production on a large scale – indeed it is this factor, together with the traumas of the Second World War, which led to the formation of the Common Market. Consequently if Fiat or Peugeot or Mercedes Benz wish to produce the best car at the best price and thus compete with cars being imported from the Far East or even the Eastern bloc countries, they must necessarily export their products. Europe quickly learned to 'export or die'.

Western Europe, therefore, provided an environment in which European companies could move away from their former national outlook towards one which is very much closer to an international or global perspective. In this respect they are probably still behind the Japanese, who understood very much earlier than the rest of us that they must export and develop world markets in order to survive, but they are ahead of the Americans who have been slow in developing a global approach to branding, advertising and marketing simply because they have the world's largest and richest market quite literally in their own backyard.

In spite of this gradual Europeanisation of the national markets of Western Europe, it is interesting to note that relatively few Eurobrands lead their segments in multiple European markets, though examples of highly successful international bands which are segment leaders in multiple European markets include Nescafé soluble coffee, Colgate toothpaste, Marlboro cigarettes, Ajax window cleaner, Badedas bath additive, Knorr soup mixes, Avon cosmetics, Nivea hand cream and Schweppes mixers. Western European markets thus tend to be populated by a mix of European and global brands on the one hand, and brands which are peculiarly and determinedly national on the other. This is a situation which is likely to continue, although we feel it is likely we will see a gradual increase in international brands occupying leading positions in major segments, with national brands finding their real strength in sub-categories or particular national niches. Clearly those companies which are prepared to develop brands which can appeal across national, cultural and language barriers, and which allow for a common approach in multiple markets, are those companies which are likely to gain the most in the long term.

CONCLUSIONS

We have tried to illustrate in this chapter how certain key markets have gone about branding at the national level, and what has been done to expand these basic approaches into the international arena.

We by no means advocate the abandonment of a local approach to branding; indeed, it is the very richness of our national cultural experiences which adds immeasurable value and texture to our products. But if there is a lesson for all of us it is that successful and effective branding implies a sensitivity not only to our own local requirements, but increasingly to those of other markets to whom we wish to appeal. Sometimes our products may succeed precisely because of their idiosyncracies, for it is these that give them their distinctiveness and appeal. And sometimes they may succeed despite their idiosyncracies. But whatever the case, we as developers of brands should be keenly aware of national differences and should develop our brands from the outset to take these into account.

I would like to thank those colleagues who have assisted in the preparation of this chapter – in Tokyo, Tadamichi Harada; in Frankfurt, Manfred Gotta; in Paris, Gerard-Pierre Blanot; in New York, Chuck Brymer.

16 The Corporate Identity as the Brand

JOHN DIEFENBACH

WHAT IS CORPORATE IDENTITY?

A corporate identity programme is really nothing more than the branding and packaging of an entire company. Like all packaging, it is a way of giving shape to the contents – a way of communicating the corporate ingredients to target groups and markets. A corporate identity programme differentiates the company in a positive and memorable way; it projects the unique personality of the corporation; it positions the company in the market-place.

Therefore, like branding and packaging, corporate identity is a powerful strategic weapon – one that promotes an understanding of the corporate purpose and provides a greater clarity in communicating that purpose to important publics including customers, employees, the financial community, government, trade unions and suppliers.

That's what it does. It gives shape, it differentiates, it clarifies, it communicates, it positions. But what *is* it? How do you package a company? Is it a name, a logo? A graphic device?

It is that and much more. A corporate identity programme is essentially a 'system' – a carefully designed system of all the visual elements which serve as points of public contact. The corporate name and logo are, of course, key elements in this system, but contrary to common understanding, they are not the only elements. The modern corporation is a very complex structure, and it communicates to its public in many different ways. There is, of course, promotional media – print, electronic, direct mail. But public perceptions are formed by many other, more permanent media: for example, company-owned 'visibility assets' – headquarters and branch offices, factories, distribution facilities, retail outlets, signage, trucks and cars, personnel uniforms, business forms and stationery, product design, packaging and point-of-purchase displays.

Every company has its own unique set of these visibility assets. Collectively they form a company's visibility quotient. Banks, for example, have an enormous physical presence in the community, with their headquarters building, branch offices, signs, and now the ubiquitous Automatic Teller Machines. The Bank of America, for example, links over 1000 branches, 400 Finance America branches and some 100 overseas offices with its strong corporate identity (Plate 16.1). The resulting unity provides them with a powerful communications synergy that might otherwise have been lost. Manufacturers, on the other hand, are not as visible, but their identities are projected beyond the factory and distribution sites through product and packaging design, trucks and cars, sales people, business forms, and corporate literature such as annual reports. Allied Van Lines, with a restricted advertising capability, discovered that by 'branding' its 11 000 vans with a strong corporate identity, it could increase consumer awareness with an estimated 22.6 billion annual impressions. In other service industries, such as restaurant chains, it is obvious that the media *is* the message. The restaurant units themselves are really three-dimensional corporate identity systems, the menu offerings being just one part of an integrated consumer experience.

All corporations and companies have public contact points, and taken together they form a network of 'permanent media' that can be used very effectively to communicate to their various publics. But to do so they must be subjected to a design discipline and integrated into a carefully orchestrated system.

A well-integrated, visual communications system uses repetition of design or its elements of colour, line and texture, to reinforce a total impression on the public memory. The logo prominently displayed in an office makes a good strong statement, but it is the echoing of its colours or a 'secondary format' on a product or package, or on the business forms, or in employee uniforms, that provides the all important, if subtle, reinforcement.

Airline customers, for example, who are impressed with the graphics painted on a 747 must not be allowed to forget that airline's identity once they enter the cabin. A good visual communications system will remind them over and over again of the company's unique personality. They may not be conscious of each detail – that the carpeting picks up the secondary corporate colour, or that the china and linen bear the same border trim used on signs at the boarding gate. They may not be aware that the typeface in the company advertising is repeated on their boarding pass, ticket holder and baggage tag, but each integrated 'item' will contribute to an overall impression of the personality unique to that airline (Plates 16.2a,b).

A company that successfully employs these visual communications techniques is perceived with more confidence. The system projects a tone of planned cohesiveness, a, reassuring sense of order. That alone strikes a responsive chord in customers. Without knowing why, they are impressed with the company's 'togetherness'. And this reflects, of course, on their products or services. Products become an extension of the corporate personality; services become less abstract, more tangible.

IDENTITY AND IMAGE

Very frequently 'identity' is confused with 'image'. They are related concepts, but they are not the same. An *image* is the *perception* that the public has of a company. It is the cumulative result of many different influences such as quality of products and management, price range, advertising style, status in the community – and permanent media. An image exists in the public's mind. *Identity*, on the other hand, is the objective reality. It is the corporation as it actually exists in the real world. It is the soul of the corporation, the sum of its parts, its goals and direction, its attitudes, its values, its corporate culture.

The goal of a corporate identity *system*, therefore is to distil and communicate the reality to the public. This can only be achieved after in-depth analysis of the nature and strategic aims of the company, and after thorough research into the nature of the public's perceptions of the company. All too often identity and image are very different. The purpose of a corporate identity programme is to close the gap, to sharpen the identity focus so it may be clearly and forcefully projected to the public.

It must be remembered, however, that marketing strategies vary greatly from company to company. In some cases corporate identity is the dominant means of communication; and in other cases a company depends heavily on individual product or service brands to carry the message to the public. Therefore, an identity programme must be devised to match the corporation's marketing strategy. There are four different types of communication strategies which manifest themselves in four different types of identity systems:

(1) Corporate dominant system
(2) Brand dominant system
(3) Balanced system
(4) Mixed system

The corporate dominant system is one in which the corporation itself is the main communicator of the marketing message. It is found in large institutional business and service organisations where the company behind the product provides the required credibility. A restaurant or department store must use a corporate identity system to express its unique personality simply because it is the sum total of its tangible impressions. These are 'single entity' companies. If it were not for carefully orchestrated identity systems they would melt into that grey world of commodity anonymity. They depend on a strong corporate identity for value-added differentation. Not only do they differentiate themselves with a strong corporate identity programme, but they also actually use a visual communication system to reshape and redefine themselves to appeal to specific market segments. When Red Lobster Inns of America found the eating habits of its customers changing to lighter, fresher, healthier foods, it not only changed its menus, but changed nearly everything – interior and exterior design, graphics, signage, uniforms, table-settings, food displays. In short, it modified its identity to accommodate the new dynamics of the market (Plates 16.3a,b).

As might be expected, a brand dominant system is one in which the individual brands are dominant, and the corporation behind them is subordinate (sometimes anonymous) in most communications. Many large consumer products companies fall into this classification (Plate 16.4).

A balanced system is one in which the corporation and its brands are given about equal weight in communications. And a mixed system is one in which the corporation is sometimes dominant and the brands are sometimes dominant. Naturally, balanced or mixed identity systems imply deliberate handling – not confusion.

It frequently happens that, under the pressure of change and other external or internal forces, an identity strategy itself undergoes change. There are many examples of corporate companies becoming brand dominant. There are even cases when a dominant brand will replace the corporate identity. An example is Consolidated Food's recent name change to the Sara Lee Corporation. In the last few years, the rapidly escalating costs of media have forced the opposite tactic. There are many more examples of brand dominant companies turning to a corporate dominant strategy – using the power of a strong corporate name to endorse or 'superbrand' many of their products, both old and new.

Whatever the strategy, clearly, it is important for management to exert control over its identity so it will be most beneficial and least disruptive, in relation not only to external publics, but to the internal corporate culture as well. There are times, however, when identity wear-out, or breakdown, can occur. Change is usually the cause.

CHANGE, THE ONLY CONSTANT

Business is always subject to external pressures, one important one being change. Change is a constant and may result from new life-styles, new markets, regulatory change, new technologies, economic forces, new competition, or simply growth and acquisition. Companies change. Markets change. Strategies, therefore, must change.

Response to change is the key. The Darwinian concept, 'Adapt or die', applies to corporate as well as biological life.

Business, of course, must respond to change if it is to survive. The response may be the development of new business or new business combinations, new organisations or organisational structures, new products, new channels of distribution, mergers and acquisitions and the like.

Once a corporation has responded to change it often finds its identity seriously altered. Deregulation in both banking and the airline industries has made many old geographical-oriented identities obsolete. Many companies have found it necessary to communicate a new identity to their publics in order to free them from old restrictions (Plate 16.5).

The transmission of the identity message is also subject to external pressures, among them: competitive forces, distribution requirements, media requirements, economic pressures, corporate requirements, regulatory requirements, etc.

Often, the result of such pressures is the homogenisation of products and services; they achieve parity with one another and all seem alike to the public. Another result may be confusion, or lack of clarity, in the image. Or perhaps the image is simply no longer accurate.

When the projected identity changes or goes out of focus it results in an inaccurate or blurred image in the public mind. It is then necessary to correct the identity system so it will again have the proper influence on the image. Or, it may be a signal to re-examine the company's marketing strategy to see if it is still the right one.

Research and analysis play a pivotal part in this reassesment. It not only helps evaluate the existing image, but also directs changes in strategy, guides the development of a new strategic identity programme, and monitors its effectiveness.

The result of all this research, analysis, and refocusing is a corporate identity programme which truly reflects the current nature and direction of the company – a design system which fuses corporate identity and public perceptions – a new branded package copious enough to contain and position the entire corporation. It can then be used to communicate to all of the company's publics – both in the business community, and in the market-place.

THE CORPORATE BRAND – COMMUNICATING IDENTITY TO THE BUSINESS COMMUNITY

Companies sell more than products or services to the ultimate consumers. They sell the corporation itself to prospective employees, to banks and brokers, to other corporations, to local, state, and federal agencies, to labour unions.

Therefore, in a very real way the company itself is an end product. It is clear that the perceptions of these publics are extraordinarily important to its well being. Even a corporation with a brand dominant strategy aimed at the market-place will find it essential to have a clear and forceful corporate identity programme with which to communicate to these secondary but very important publics.

As corporations grow by creating or acquiring new divisions and subsidiaries, they often do so at the expense of a once clearly understood identity.

It doesn't take long before a company can no longer be contained in its old identity package. Even management can become confused. It is here that a well thought out corporate identity system can be of enormous help. The demanding process behind the creation of the system forces management to re-evaluate direction and purpose, and leads it through a 'decision tree' which helps it achieve that delicate balance between corporate dominance on the one hand, and divisional or subsidiary autonomy, on the other. The emerging visual identity system takes into account the precise amount of individual visibility and identity that is desirable for each division or subsidiary and 'tiers' it in a system ensuring the right amount of corporate identification.

Because an identity system is visual it allows both management and interested publics to 'see' the company as a whole. And it allows divisional and subsidiary employees to see exactly where they fit into the larger scheme of things. Because a visual identity programme is a distillation of the corporate 'position' or strategic goal it is an invaluable managerial aid: if the strategy is confused or off base, it will literally show up in the design itself.

It doesn't take long for an untended identity to become choked by a jungle of names, logos, brands, sub-brands, subsidiary and divisional identities. The resulting identity blur is not only confusing to potential investors, employees, suppliers or retailers, but represents a tremendous loss of synergy as well. Each and every corporate acitvity should be both contributing to, and receiving benefit from, a highly charged corporate identity.

CORPORATE BRAND – COMMUNICATING IDENTITY TO THE MARKET-PLACE

It is easy to see how corporate identity works as a brand in the service industries. As we have shown, financial institutions, retailers, restaurants, insurance companies, airlines are by their nature corporate dominant. Their identity and product are one and the same.

But what about a brand-dominant corporation – a company that takes great pride in its ability to create strong individual product brands? Surely it doesn't find any advantage in a strong corporate identity. Not true. Any corporation must, as discussed above, communicate with the business community on a corporation to corporation level. Therefore there is always a need for a strong corporate identity programme. It is just that its identity may not always be directed at the consumer.

But that is changing. Corporate identity is coming into its own even in the land of the brand, sub-brand and branded line extension. In the past the whole marketing process was built around the concept of brand management, with highly specific products managed at middle levels of corporations. Today, more and more brands are managed at high levels by dominant presidents. And often the result is 'superbranding' – an increasing reliance on the power of the equity found in a well-managed corporate identity.

What is superbranding? It is a form of umbrella marketing whereby a corporation 'borrows' the equity it has accrued at great expense in its corporate name, and applies it to a new product or line. A superbrand implies instant recognition and high acceptance – intensified, on-shelf impact and sharp consumer focus. Honda, Dole, Birds Eye, Stouffer's, Del Monte, and Levis, are just some of the companies that come to mind which have achieved superbrand status over the years (Plate 16.6). The superbrand identity may be used alone with a description such as Honda *Power Equipment* or as an endorsement for another line bearing its own separate brand identity, as in Stouffer's *Lean Cuisine* frozen entrées, or Pillsbury *Hungry Jack* biscuits. In either case, the new product borrows heavily from the equity already built into the superbrand or corporate identity.

Superbranding is not merely the addition of an endorsement. It is a serious shift in strategic thinking, leading to careful re-evaluation of product management and presentation. Superbranding is becoming a marketing imperative. Why? Simply because today's intensified competition and escalating marketing costs make it necessary to use the stored kinetic energy of a pre-sold identity. It works two ways: first, superbranding greatly reduces the need for the excessive media exposure usually required when introducing an unknown product. The already familiar identity 'flags down' consumer attention much more efficiently than a totally unfamiliar one. Secondly, superbranding neatly sidesteps consumer scepticism without diluting curiosity and excitement by deftly blending novelty and familiarity. The tension created by these two apparent contradictions makes the product even more memorable.

Furthermore, any special introductory advertising done by the company for any new product will perform a double function. It will supercharge the introduction with a powerpack of corporate equity; and it will also strengthen consumer awareness of all other existing brands. This 'double duty' media usage produces a synergistic effect adding up to more than the sum spent on individual or isolated campaigns.

In introducing a new product, the trick in superbranding is to establish the proper relationship between the new brand identity and the familiar superbrand or corporate identity. Package design must employ all the devices it can to appeal to the consumer's curiosity and sense of adventure by emphasising the newness and unique qualities of the product. But it must not allow the familiar superbrand to overwhelm the product's own individual personality. But, on the other hand, it must use the accepted and easily retained superbrand name to flag the consumer's attention and to reassure him that the product will meet his expectations. The product must be both the 'same' and 'other', both 'new' and 'familiar'.

A good example of design resolving this tension is Stouffer's frozen foods.

The company wanted to introduce a line of ten low-calorie frozen entrées to appeal to the growing 'diet conscious' market. While this could have been accomplished by merely extending the existing line and adding a banner announcing 'reduced in calories', management felt that such an approach lacked the excitement generated by a whole new product. At the same time, and given today's media costs, it made good sense to use the superbrand status of the corporate identity – Stouffer's, a powerful marketing tool synonymous with quality frozen foods (Plate 16.7).

The solution was to invent a new brand and superbrand it with the corporate identity. The graphics, background colour and appetising photography created a distinctive look for the new line, and yet the overall feeling was familiar. Then, to flag attention to the product, the Stouffer's name and logo were placed in a secondary format in a prominent but not dominant position. The use of colour, and properly weighted design elements moved the consumer's eye in a proscribed path, first reassuring with the familiar, then exciting with the unexpected.

Superbrands not only command consumer attention, the also encourage retailers to devote more linear feet of shelf space to the line. Birds Eye is an excellent example of how a strong corporate presence can help dominate the retail setting. With over 200 different individual packages in various product lines, categories and sublines, it is essential for Birds Eye to convince store owners to devote as much space as possible to as many products as possible. It is easy to see how superbrand clout can be invaluable. If it were not for a strong corporate identity, many of the sublines might go begging.

Point-of-purchase dominance is further aided by a well-designed superbrand identity system by creating a strong repeat pattern – a *gestalt* effect – right on the shelves.

More and more marketing managers are learning to appreciate the use of corporate identity as a brand or superbrand. They know that its proper application can save millions of media pounds and dollars today, and, at the same time, build corporate brand equity with each campaign, guaranteeing even more marketing strength for a competitive tomorrow.

LAST WORDS

This chapter began with the simple statement that a corporate identity programme is nothing more than the branding and packaging of an entire company. That is true. But it should be clear by now that 'nothing more' is quite a bit. As any brand manager knows, a product's name and packaging are critical to its success. Successful identity management – for that's what branding really is – is no simple matter. It depends on a thorough understanding of the product and its consumer benefits as well as a research-backed analysis of the market segment it wishes to reach. Since brand identity truly positions a product in the market-place, it is essential that it is sharply focused and properly aimed.

The same is true of corporate identity. The process behind the creation of a strong visual identity is no simple matter. A well-defined and clearly expressed identity is always the result of intense corporate soul-searching. It demands a good hard look at the company's organisational make-up, a painstaking analysis of its strategic thrust, and a concise articulation of its goals and purpose. On the other side of the equation, the creation of an identity programme requires a keen awareness of how the company is actually perceived by its various publics.

The packaging of a corporation differs from product packaging only in complexity. A company's 'ingredients' are more difficult to isolate and define. And in place of one market segment, it has many different publics to reach – the business community, government, labour, as well as its consumer market. These difficulties are overcome by means of a pathfinding process which leads management through the corporate maze, and market research which allows management to see the company as their customers see it.

Corporate identity is much more than a differentiating device, much more than a 'signature'. Properly orchestrated as a complete visual system it has the power to position the company and its products, improve employee morale, communicate to investors and suppliers, clarify, divisional and subsidiary participation, offer management a tool with which to measure and compare strategic opinions, and marshal the impressive forces of permanent media.

That's a lot to get out of one package.

17 Organising for New Product Development

ROBERT GRAYSON

NATURE OF ORGANISATION

The discipline of management teaches us that we need to follow a definite sequence of steps for the successful completion of any human endeavour. These steps are:

(1) defining the objectives and scope of the project;
(2) promulgating the policies necessary to achieve those objectives;
(3) organising in a logical and workable manner so as to fix responsibility and facilitate achievement of the objectives;
(4) developing a plan;
(5) applying of techniques and skills to satisfactorily complete the assignments; and
(6) controlling and measuring the results.

As we examine the new product process, we see that it is the third step above that addresses the problem of organisation directly while step six does so obliquely. Without a proper structure there may be duplication of effort, inadequate attention to certain functions, rivalry and friction among personnel, and delays in decision-making.

Yet it is generally recognised that organisation problems are among the most perplexing confronting modern managements. It is an accepted fact that the segregation of responsibility, elimination of uncertainty, and specialisation by function are bare minimum requirements for attaining a significant degree of efficiency. What is not realised is the extent to which business concerns actually tolerate improper organisation. Illogical arrangements often develop and continue in spite of their adverse effect.

The rapidly changing nature of most business activities presents an additional problem for corporate organisers. A plan that was satisfactory at one time may become obsolete within a short time, not necessarily because the nature of the business or its functions have changed, but because the environment has shifted. Therefore, organising to perform the company's work should be a dynamic function for management.

However, there is no one right way to organise a corporation. Indeed, many survive in spite of a poor organising plan or even the lack of a plan altogether.

The extent of elaborateness of structure, of levels of directive authority, of delegation from the top, and decentralisation of responsibility are all issues about which there are genuine differences of view among equally discerning theorists and practitioners. Nevertheless, among the writers in the field of management there is general agreement regarding the handling of specialised functions. And the new product development is one of the most specialised.

Organisation Planning

Organisation planning is, figuratively or actually, segregating those activities that most logically fit together for effective execution of the enterprise. One must consider, among other things, the nature of the work, the degree of specialisation, duplication within the organisation, sources of information – both residual and ongoing, reporting relationships, and labour allocation and development. At all times the achievement of efficiency is measured against the objectives of the enterprise. However, organisation is a means to an end, merely one of the tools for accomplishing the company's objectives; it should not be allowed to become an end in itself.

Defining Organisation

The basic structure of a corporation is the organisational form familiarly known as a hierarchy. This is the well-known arrangement of boxes, with the most important executives at the top and two, three, or more subordinates in boxes one level down.

An organisation should not be considered to be people. It is a facilitating mechanism. The organisation chart is the corporate roadmap but it too is not the organisation. The formal organisation structure is the directed division of the physical activities and decision-making activities into subsections and then the total integration of these segments into a chain of command.

In simple terms, organisation is the structure required for carrying out the plans of the enterprise. It is the establishment of relationships among the various components of the company so all are related and combined into an effective unit which may then be directed toward the achievement of common objectives. It is the manager's function to see that the work is arranged in such a manner that maximum efficiency can be achieved.

FUNCTIONAL ORGANISATION THEORY

Definition

The functional plan is the traditional plan of organisation and is most common in industry. Essentially, it consists merely of carrying out the principles of the division of labour into the realm of management.

Under the functional plan problems of organisation are simplified. For example, all factories of a given type report to a single executive or all new product development work is co-ordinated by a single department, which, with proper staff, is in a position to standardise policies, methods, facilities, procedures, and so on. That is, the corporate body is made up of separate units each carrying out its own function which contributes to the well-being and efficiency of the whole.

It is frequently felt that a good executive can make almost any kind of organisation run. This point is not disputed. Rather, put the finest personnel into a poor organisation and the resulting friction, duplication of effort, unnecessary co-ordinating committees, frequency of formalised internal communications, and other problems will slowly but surely drain the company of its vitality and, subsequently, its profits while it may still look as if it is being run well.

Specialisation: A Refinement of Function

The purpose of specialisation (or division of work) is to produce more and better work with the same effort. Managers who are always concerned with the same matters acquire ability, sureness and accuracy which increases their output. The concept of specialisation, though simple, forms the underpinnings of proper organisation. It provides the opportunity for maximum output with minimum slippage within the organisation. Additionally, responsibility for performance can be clearly delineated, rewarded or punished, as the case may be.

If the development of new products is indeed a specialised function, there seems to be strong support for taking this function out of the mainstream of daily activity to get the maximum benefits from specialisation.

THE BASIC ORGANISATIONS FOR NEW-PRODUCT DEVELOPMENT

The most Common Structure: Brand Management within the Line Organisation

In most companies new products are developed by the regular line organisation and handled either by a product manager, who also has responsibility for existing brands (see Figure 17.1), or by a product manager, whose sole responsibility is for new products (see Figure 17.2).

In the first case, if existing brands require work, these will get the time and attention of the product manager. And that is how it should be. After all, it is the current brands that pay the bills. Additionally, there is generally no real incentive for the product manager to bring a new product to market early, or even on time for that matter. Managers do not get bonuses for being early and they generally do not get fired either for being late. As a consequence, new-product development will suffer. (Note: One of the first things most practising management consultants look at when searching for under-achieving performance is the reward system. In this case, however, a bonus for early market entry might be counterproductive, as the brand manager would most likely take time away from the current business.)

Moreover, a product manager tends to have a narrow view of the world. He or she is generally confined to a small area of the market-place, with the result

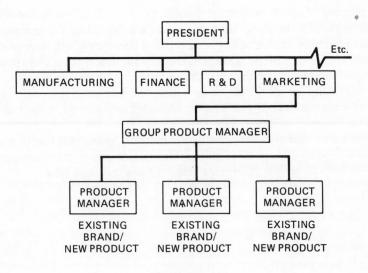

FIGURE 17.1

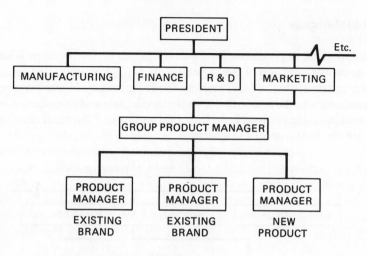

FIGURE 17.2

that new products will not be particularly innovative. Thus, a product manager working on the Campbell Soup brands would be quite capable of developing a new flavour of soup but could hardly be expected to develop frozen puff-pastry sandwiches – nor should he be! Even so, it is most common to assign a new product project to product managers in addition to ongoing brands.

Where a specialist new-product manager (see Figure 17.2) is the focus of development, he or she operates under the direction of a group product manager. Thus the bottleneck moves up to the GPM level. The 'groupie' is responsible for so many going brands that he or she has even less time than a product manager to devote to new products, even though this manager may have broader experience. If you understand the pressure that develops when a major competitor introduces a product against the GPM's most profitable brand, you can realise that a new product, with potential profits two or three years hence, will be pushed aside. Of course, the same would apply if the new product manager reported directly to a line marketing vice-president.

Given the flaws in this type of organisation, one wonders why it is so frequently employed. The explanation is simple. In this model, no visible cost is associated with new product development because, if the product management salaries are being paid for by the going brands, the new products ride free, at least from the budgeting end. The unfortunate fact is that most managers do not consider that a day's delay today will almost surely result in a day's delay at the project end which, for a successful product, means a delay in new profits. For example, the cost (pre-tax) of one day's delay for a $10 million new product with 10 per cent net margin is $3205.13 (assuming a six-day selling week).

The R&D Structure

Another popular organisation for the development of new products is having them under the direction of R&D (see Figure 17.3). For a hundred years this was the system within AT&T, and the resulting paucity of market-oriented new products was the major factor in the development of competition in the telecommunications industry. At least that was one of the main reasons put forth for the break-up of the system.

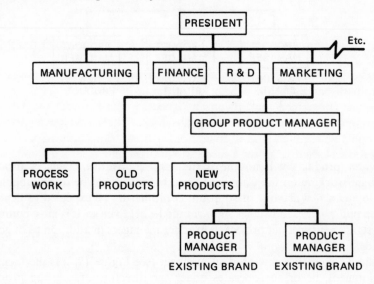

FIGURE 17.3

Management's concern with this structure should be twofold. First, products may be developed that are not suitable for the market-place. Even the most customer/consumer-oriented marketing departments often bring out products that are rejected. Therefore, you have to consider the increased odds against success by an organisation whose orientation is technical/development.

The second concern is that the reward system for research and development personnel is generally structured around publications, patents and papers delivered at technical meetings. Thus, one would expect some subconscious effort to be placed in that direction, often to the detriment of market-oriented, consumer-satisfying goods.

The Task Force Structure

Task forces (see Figure 17.4) are also popular, but they suffer from one serious drawback – a lack of continuity. In working on new products, one acquires a

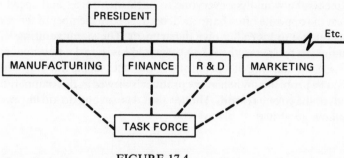

FIGURE 17.4

special expertise which takes many years to sharpen, but task forces are generally disbanded at the conclusion of the task.

Also, it is assumed that anyone assigned to a task force is capable of performing new product tasks. This just is not so. There is a type of creativity (combined with a high level of tolerance for frustration) that marks a good new product executive. Often a successful product manager on a going brand is moved into new product development for a broadening of the experience required for promotion, only to fail because opposite skills are required: ideas versus numbers: strategic versus tactical skill; the excitement of uncharted waters versus the comparative safety of the known.

Task forces should not be confused with venture groups. This latter organisation is generally a permanent group which, having developed a concept or product for a new business, maintains its corpus and becomes an operating group. If a group's function is to develop a new product/concept and then to pass it along to an existing group, it is essentially operating as a New Product Department (see below).

The Committee Structure

The 'president's committee' (see Figure 17.5) concept is not as popular as it once was, and that is fortunate. It was based on the notion that if the president appointed a high-level group composed of top-ranking members of various

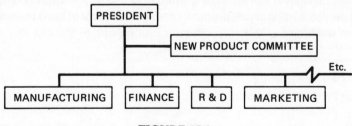

FIGURE 17.5

departments, he would get everyone to back the project and speed it on its way. Just the opposite often happened, because each member of the committee was answerable to his or her own department. The manufacturing VP would see production problems; the R&D VP would envision development problems (along with the shelving of a pet project); the Sales Department would discern distribution problems. When a new product is viewed in this manner, it is often rejected for the wrong reasons. Hidden agendas can and do kill any project, no matter how good it is.

What, then is the ideal organisation for new product development?

In some companies it is known merely as the New Product Department. (Note: A proprietary study conducted for the purpose of ascertaining the most efficient organisation for directing corporate product policy and new product development indicated that companies with new product departments *per se* developed 63 per cent more new products than those whose products were developed within the line organisation.) More advanced companies have, however, come to realise that a much broader rôle is required (see Figure 17.6).

The functions of the New Product Department are threefold: first to develop new products; second, to weed out from the existing line those products that no longer are contributing as measured by the company's predetermined standards; and third, to advise on the product line rationalisation/synergy for acquisitions.

New Products Development

For all the reasons discussed at the beginning of this chapter, management theory strongly supports the concept of new products being developed as a specialised function. The three main benefits of this approach are:

(1) a clearly placed responsibility not diluted by the need to make current profit projections;
(2) the continuing nature of the task and its cumulative learning effect; and
(3) objective appraisal of opportunities.

It would be expected that once a product is ready for launch it would be turned over to the line organisation. Experience has shown that if there was an assistant working on the new product, it is often wise to transfer this person along with the product to ensure continuity.

Existing Product Analysis

Very few line managers are capable of being objective when it comes to

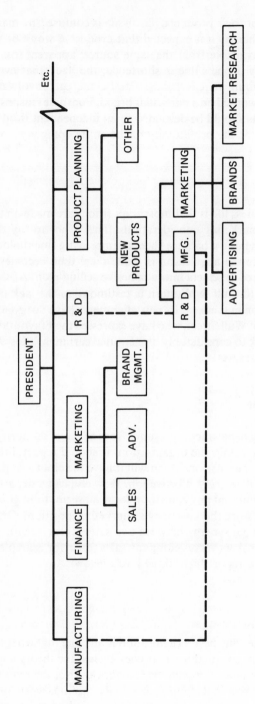

FIGURE 17.6

discontinuing one of their products. The issue is confused by many factors: 'full-line theory', whereby it is expected that product B won't be sold unless product A is also available from the same source; apparent loss of stature within the company if one's line is shortened; the 'fact' that even a losing product can contribute to overheads; finally, the ego involvement for a manager who once worked on a particular brand. For these reasons the task of eliminating products should be delegated to an independent third party, one that is responsible for the profitability of the entire company's offerings.

Acquisitions

The sad fact of business life is that most acquisitions are made on the basis of financial and not marketing considerations. This is not to say that we are opposed to strengthening a balance sheet or improving stockholders' equity, but rather that once the acquisition is made there then becomes a need to integrate the acquired products into a cohesive selling plan. At this date the unconglomerating of Gulf & Western is testimony to the lack of attention given to this function in the past. Its new alignments have not gone unnoticed by the gunslingers of Wall Street, who have expressed their favourable opinion by bidding the stock to considerably higher price/earnings ratios. At last G & W is getting some respect.

Problems in Camelot

A product-planning department can suffer from a lack of authority if it is not positioned properly within the organisation. It should report directly to the company president, because only then will it have the clout – in time, money and personnel – to do a truly effective job. How else can a department head convince the president that an acquisition for what seems to be good financial reasons will really hurt the company's marketing position? Or that what appears to be potential synergy between two sales forces is really a potential conflict – grocery brokers versus company sales force, for example. Certainly not by sending up a report from three levels below!

SUMMARY

For many companies the 'best' organisation is any one that works. However, to attempt to operate in a manner that goes against the theory and empirical evidence of good organisation may be foolhardy. Also, the wrong organisation, while not apparent in its failure, can do its insidious work, much like an undetected cancer, causing the company to suboptimise growth and profitability.

Fortunately, a re-examination of corporate structure need not be done more often than biannually. Thus the task should be neither onerous nor boring. However, if it isn't done with this regularity, an opportunity to improve corporate performance may be missed.

18 The Future of Branding

KLAUS MORWIND

INTRODUCTION

As noted in earlier chapters, several trends external to the branded goods industry are likely to have an important impact upon its development: the increased globalisation of industries and products, the advent and growth of the services industry and, particularly in advanced Western societies, a move away from manufacturing industry.

However, we contend that the greatest impact upon the branded goods industry will be created by the *internal* management decisions and policies of those firms operating on a *worldwide* basis. We believe that, in time, these worldwide entities will increasingly dominate their markets locally, regionally and internationally, often at the expense of smaller firms that operate only on a local, a regional or multinational basis.

THE GROWTH IN WORLDWIDE COMPETITION

In spite of short-term political and economic setbacks, the trend towards an increasing international division of labour, and with it growing international trade, is likely to continue uninterrupted. During the past ten years, international trade has expanded at a rate in excess of 10 per cent per year, while the world GNP has increased only 3 per cent per year. By replacing the manpower and production facilities of more highly developed and more costly nations, the countries of Southeast Asia and Latin America are forcing this development. However, if the advanced industrial countries adopt the policy of investing in lesser developed countries to aid their development and capability to contribute to world GNP, as was the case earlier in Japan, the overall end result will be a strengthening of both international trade and world production (GNP).

International trade is not a new phenomenon; however, it is a changing phenomenon. In the last twenty years, in addition to the growth of world trade, we have seen an ever expanding interlocking of world economic relationships. Companies are developing which are truly global companies. An example of the importance of the international/worldwide relationships can be found in West Germany. Here approximately 60 per cent of industrial workers are employed in the international sector – 16 per cent of these in companies with a financial interest overseas, and 44 per cent in companies with foreign manufacturing facilities or foreign subsidiaries.

INCREASED COMPLEXITY IN WORLD TRADE

The contribution of global companies to global production and sales has risen more rapidly than the growth rate of international trade. However, the further interlocking of world economic relationships is not only reflected in the growth of the global companies' share of the world's total GNP, but also in the growing worldwide activities of the tertiary (or services) sector – in particular, the increasing rôle of business, legal and tax consultancies. The importance of this tertiary sector to the interlocking relationship process can be seen in four relatively recent developments:

(1) The strengthening of trade protection measures and the implementation of ecology protection measures.
(2) A media explosion resulting in
    (a) international delivery of printed and electronic media, exemplified by the European or American editions for the printed media and use of satellites for television, and
    (b) a trend towards extreme segmentation of target audiences, reflected in a dramatic increase in special magazines and growth of cable television.
(3) An audience of consumers, aided by consumption of better segmented and targeted media and greater use of international travel, that today and more so in the future are well-informed, critical and knowledgeable.
(4) A tendency on the part of the less powerful and poorer countries to organise themselves into formal groupings to encourage trade, mutual support and free movement of labour.

It is apparent that companies will have to address these four issues increasingly if they are to survive the pressures of competition in the markets of the world. However, only a relatively few companies, generally those that dominate their fields, currently demonstrate that they have acquired the necessary capabilities to address these key issues and hence compete successfully in world markets.

Moreover, as these capabilities require both know-how and significant financial resources, the dominant global firms are likely to continue to increase their share of world markets.

TODAY'S CONSUMER: SIMILAR TASTES DESPITE NATIONAL BORDERS

Aiding global companies to address markets worldwide is the increased tendency for consumers to have similar needs, interests and tastes, despite cultural and national boundaries. Owing to improving worldwide communications and faster information exchange, actual distances and boundaries seem to be of less significance. Factors which cause social stratification, such as education and the extent of urbanisation, are becoming increasingly similar from country to country and feature more than nationality in explaining differing consumer needs.

Growing segmentation, *across* international and world markets, is stimulated by both manufacturers and consumers. Improving standards of living and education, the increased awareness in what we eat, drink and wear and the reduction in political interest are powerful consumer forces causing a movement in this direction. The desire by international manufacturers to promote sales of products, created for small demographic target groups, by offering them internationally is a further driving force in this process. In short, while the world's consumers are being ever more segmented into social demographic target groups by various manufacturers, these groups themselves are becoming more alike from one country to another, despite national and cultural borders.

This trend forms the basis of a move towards the greater fragmentation of markets, or what futurist John Naisbitt calls a 'Multiple Option Society' – a society with an ever increasing range of choices and options. This has, in turn, placed even more pressure on manufacturers to market new products, either to expand market share or simply to compensate for declining brands.

One result of this ever increasing segmentation process has been that manufacturers are faced with rising costs for products which are becoming more specialised and designed for ever smaller, more discrete segments. If this trend continues we will have come full circle away from mass production, back to more flexible, high quality, small-scale methods of production.

Despite current efforts to develop flexible, cost-efficient manufacturing systems (e.g. robotisation), probably the only way in which companies will be able to enjoy both the advantages of mass production, and yet still be able to meet the requirements of more segmented markets, will be to adopt a global approach to marketing. In the future, highly fragmented national markets can, and probably must, become merely a part of global market segments, serviceable by companies prepared to utilise significant know-how and financial strength to sell the same or similar products through a worldwide marketing system.

THE PURCHASE DECISION: MORE CHOICES, MORE RISKS, MORE METHODS

The greater range of choice and selection brought on both by manufacturers' efforts to offer more demographically targeted products and by consumers' desire to acquire them, inevitably leads to increasingly complex purchase decisions. To overcome these, while still allowing for the many factual and psychological factors involved in such decisions, consumers today must rely more upon brand reputations as a base source for information. Purchasers must use a buying pattern that involves selecting brand names. The fact that this is already happening helps explain why, in many categories, brand loyalty is rising and why repurchase rates are often very high, despite the great range of choice.

We note, however, that this relatively 'irrational' purchase behaviour is not evident in all product categories. For more important purchases, the consumer makes his decision in a rational manner, following an information gathering stage and careful consideration. For less important, and often more frequent, purchases, the decision is made almost unconsciously. This type of 'unconscious' purchase decision can generally be made only when the product has a built-in, well-recognised positive association for the customer. Examples would include brands that effectively project an image of high performance or reliability. In short, for relatively frequently purchased categories, effective branding can carry a series of messages that the consumer uses to reduce the complexity of the purchase analysis and thereby achieve an almost unconscious decision.

This type of purchase decision is often achieved today in sectors where branding was previously little used, or which were considered to be commodity sectors. For example, one used to purchase tennis shoes or sneakers, but today Adidas or Nike are bought. Instead of buying just T-shirts, today's consumers demand a crocodile patch or similar symbol.

The proliferation of own-brand or store-brand products is not in conflict with the strong move towards branding. Store brands, in a similar way to normal branded products, have for the consumer a special meaning communicated through brand labels. The so-called store brand is, therefore, only a variant of product branding.

In summary, the development of strong, well-supported brands, trademarks or labels serves both the consumer *and* the manufacturer. For the manufacturer, effective branding can lead to increased repurchase rates and brand loyalty. For the consumer, branding allows easier purchase decisions based on information communicated, sometimes almost unconsciously, through the brand image.

STRATEGIES – ALTERNATIVES FOR BRANDED GOODS INDUSTRIES

Branded goods industries should expect an evolution in two principal directions:

(1) the opening up of new opportunities for the marketing of branded goods;
(2) the increasing internationalisation of successful brands.

The driving force for these developments, aside from the previously mentioned shifts in consumer opinion and behaviour, is likely to be the need for expansion and growth to which most companies are subject. In order to survive in the long term, many companies now realise that they must strengthen their market positions, not simply on a national basis but increasingly on a global, or at least an international, scale.

Dealing with these large market aggregates can often provide a company with key advantages, primarily in the areas of marketing and manufacturing costs, which can often be decisive in intensely competitive situations. Along with the important cost benefits, there exists yet another advantage to global marketing which is rarely discussed – that of risk reduction.

Risk reduction through global marketing, the idea of selling successful concepts and brands to similar target groups across international borders, is likely to become much more important when we consider that the failure rate of new products is likely to grow as we continue to segment our markets. The mounting failure rate, combined with the increasing speed with which competition can react, should encourage corporations to consider spreading the risks of new product development and introduction across global markets. Ideally, only products with strong similarities in terms of formulation, positioning, trademarks, etc. can be efficiently marketed on a broad international basis.

BRANDING AND TRADEMARKING

In the face of a continuous growth in product availability and choice, distinctive branding and the potential it affords for spontaneous communication through labels and brand names (trademarking) promises to play a growing rôle in determining the ultimate success or failure of a product.

Trademarks, over time, develop personality traits in very much the same way as people. People with distinctive features can be described relatively easily. Consistent and precise trademark personalities can, in a like manner, become firmly impressed upon the minds of consumers and communicate a consistent and precise message.

Hence, the unity and consistency of all the features of a trademark are essential criteria for success. Consumer research has indicated that a lack of consistency and unity between the brand name, the packaging and the advertising is subconsciously recognised by the consumer and leads to a feeling of detachment, ultimately resulting in brand switching. Therefore, it is likely that techniques for uncovering these inconsistencies will be used to an even greater extent in the future and that strong trademarks will become stronger and more distinctive.

To establish a distinctive trademark and a distinctive personality it is going to become more important that products are aimed ever more precisely at clearly defined target market groups. It seems likely, therefore, that in the future, especially where new products are concerned, more emphasis will be placed on target market research to help define and develop the appropriate product personality correctly, as manifested via the brand name, packaging and advertising.

Of equal importance will be a far more precise definition of a product's advantages, be they practical and/or perceived, versus rival products. For only in the declaration of differences will corporations introducing new products provide consumers with sufficient reason to switch from the automatic or subconscious purchase decision.

INCREASING INTERNATIONALITY – THE CHALLENGE FOR BRANDING

An increasingly global brand orientation represents a considerable obstacle for the development of descriptive trademarks. There appear to be three potential solutions to the need for international trademarks.

The first is the development of descriptive or semi-descriptive names for a target market segment. These names should be sufficiently descriptive to allow those in the target group, in all target countries, to understand the description or at least to form the correct associations.

The second route is to develop brand names with no descriptive content whatsoever but which are broadly 'internationally associative' with the function, appeal or culture of the product.

The third possible approach would be to choose a brand name which is relatively neutral and non-specific. The challenge here is to give an inherently meaningless term both meaning and personality, through various advertising/communication methods.

In an ideal world, the perfect international trademark is the descriptive trademark – a name which carries its message across linguistic and cultural borders. Although a trend towards the internationalisation of linguistic codes is likely to increase considerably, it is unlikely that internationally descriptive brand names will be frequently adopted in the forseeable future. At present, this type of solution is often attempted by US corporations with only limited success. In some markets these brand names are descriptive, in others associative, while in others they merely communicate that the product is 'foreign'. However, the trend towards international segmentation strategies, together with the probable future increased comprehension of key international languages, may mean that descriptive trademarks will become increasingly important in mass markets.

Since descriptive names are often long, cumbersome and difficult to secure, the second type of trademark, with correct suggestive associations, will probably be relied on in most market sectors. This type of brand name is both more expensive and complex to establish than descriptive brand names since considerable market research is likely to be needed to ensure the correct communication nuances in those many countries (with differing languages and cultures) where the brand will be marketed.

The third type of name, those that are non-descriptive and non-associative are likely to assume a rôle of greater importance in the future because they solve the key problems inherent in the other types. Specifically, a non-descriptive, non-associative name can be used when the need for international and global marketing is strong, but when language barriers to descriptive/associative naming stand in the way.

TRADEMARKS AND THE GROWTH OF THE ENGLISH LANGUAGE

As usage of the English language spreads, it is probable that it will become the language of choice in international communications. Furthermore, the USA, which has by far the largest and richest domestic consumer market in the world, is not only a clear leader in consumer marketing but is likely to become an increasingly important factor in many areas of new product development. Therefore, if product development takes place in an English-speaking country, and if English progressively serves as an international means of communication, the English language will continue to influence the selection of trademarks, as it has in the past. It can be expected that in the future, companies which market on a global basis will use the English language for trademarks to a greater extent, whether or not their base language is English.

Those who might feel that the projected future importance of the English language represents a form of national loss can draw consolidation from the fact that it will be American English – one of the most open, vibrant and alive languages in the world – that will serve as the base language for international branding. There will, of course, be very many non-English names as well. These brand names may also become absorbed into international usage and thus increase the richness and ease of international communication.

CONCLUSIONS

We are moving, after a long period of international trade, to a much more complex interlocking of world trading relationships. At the same time, consumers are becoming more discriminating in their needs and require a growing array of products and services. Moreover, this phenomenon is an international one. The result is that markets are becoming progressively segmented, yet these specific market segments show considerable similarities from one country to another. International companies have recognised these trends and are marketing well-targeted products in more and more countries in order to achieve economics of scale.

The age of international and global branding has arrived and will develop strongly in the future. Such branding requires considerable resources and skill. The rewards can be great but the risks are high. Those companies which take full account of these trends will reap the rewards of global marketing.

Index